THE LIBRARY OF PIANO CLASSICS

LARGE PRINT EDITION

EDITED BY AMY APPPLEBY

EDITORIAL ASSISTANT: JACQUELINE TORRANCE

Music Sales America

DISTRIBUTED BY

HAL•LEONARD®
CORPORATION

7777 W. BLUEMOUND RD. P.O. BOX 13819 MILWAUKEE, WI 53213

CONTENTS

Tango

Isaac Albéniz (1860–1909)

Four Pieces from The Little Notebook

Johann Sebastian Bach (1685–1750)

Minuet I

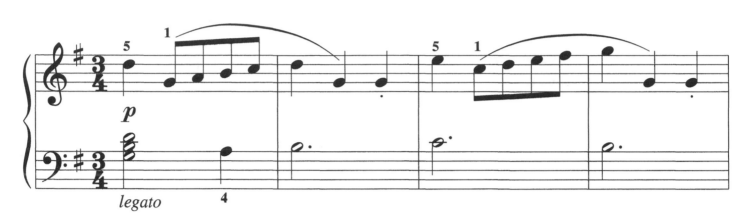

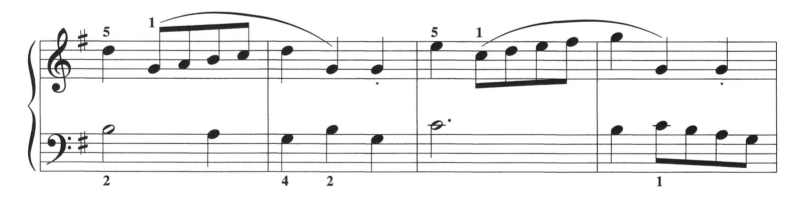

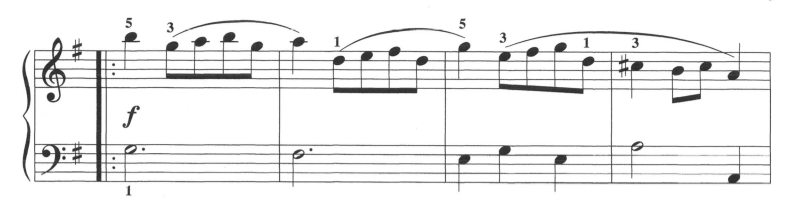

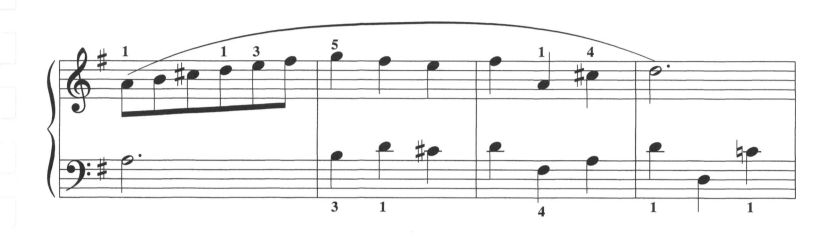

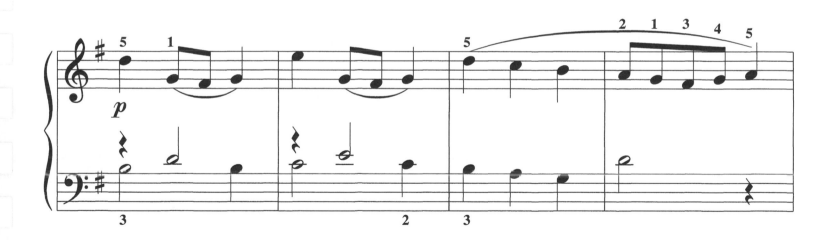

Minuet II

12

Musette

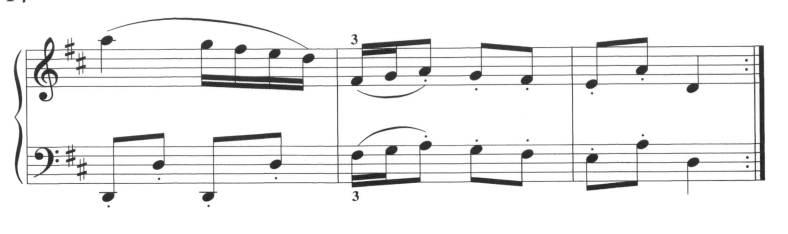

March

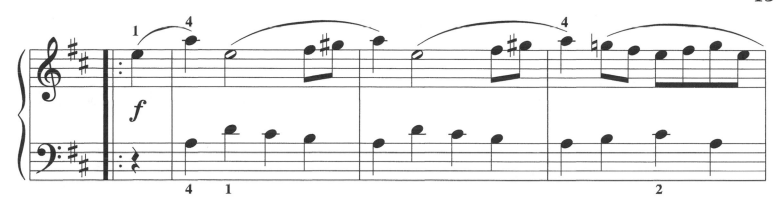

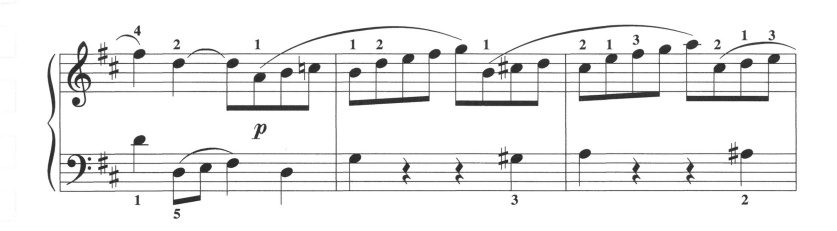

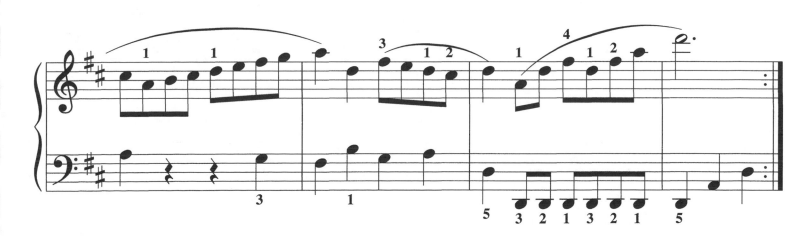

Prelude

Book 1, No. 1 from The Well-Tempered Clavier

Johann Sebastian Bach (1685–1750)

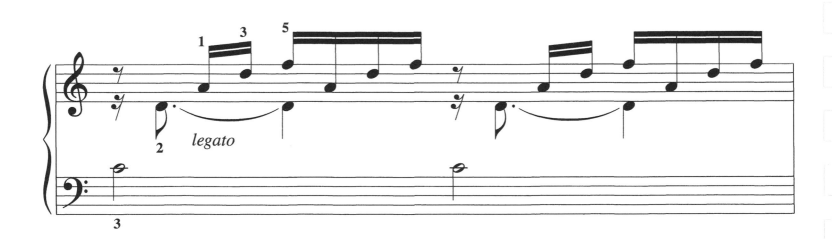

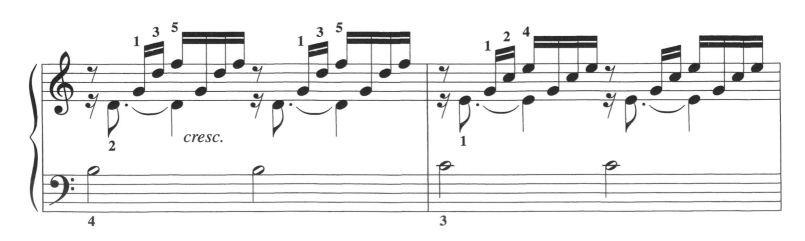

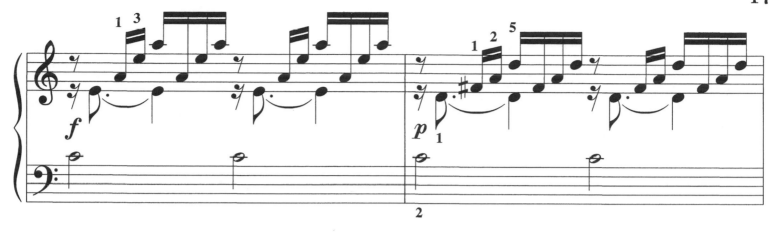

Prelude and Fugue

Book 2, No. 12 from The Well-Tempered Clavier

Johann Sebastian Bach (1685–1750)

Prelude

24

Fugue

Prelude and Fugue

Book 1, No. 2 from The Well-Tempered Clavier

Johann Sebastian Bach (1685–1750)

Prelude

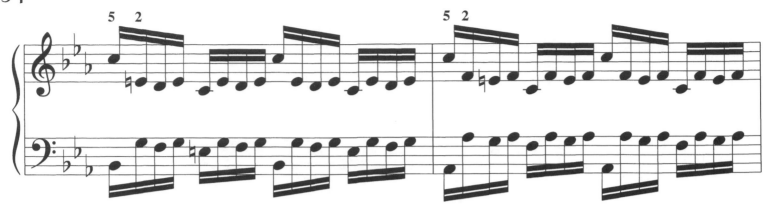

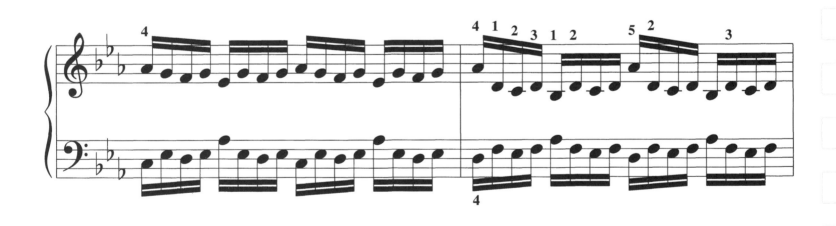

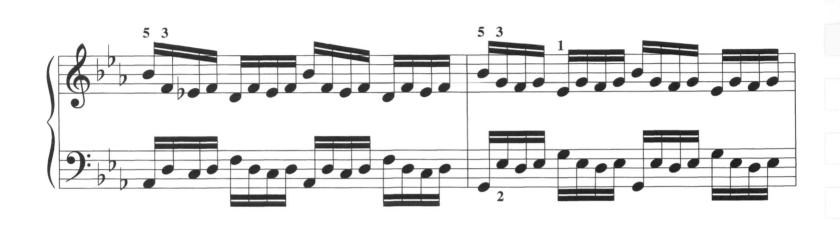

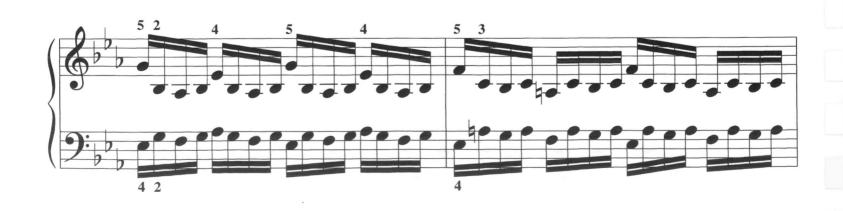

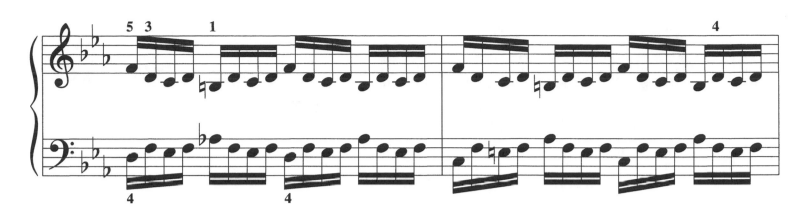

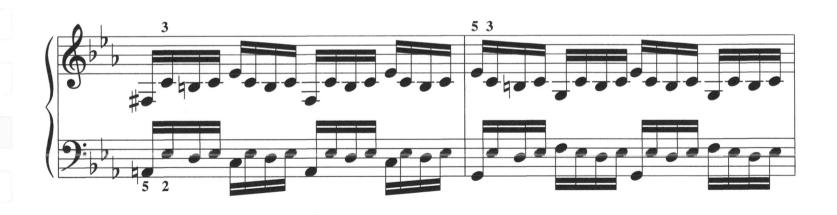

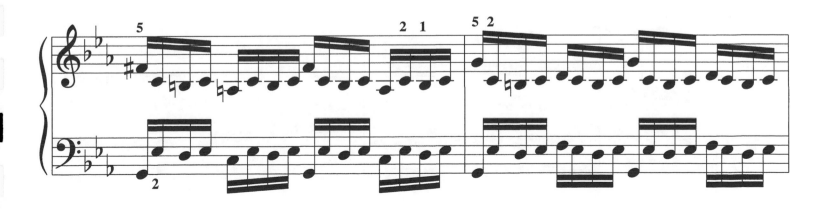

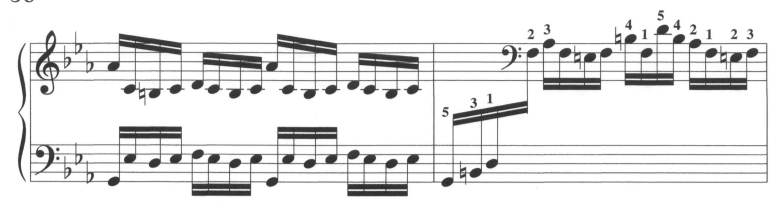

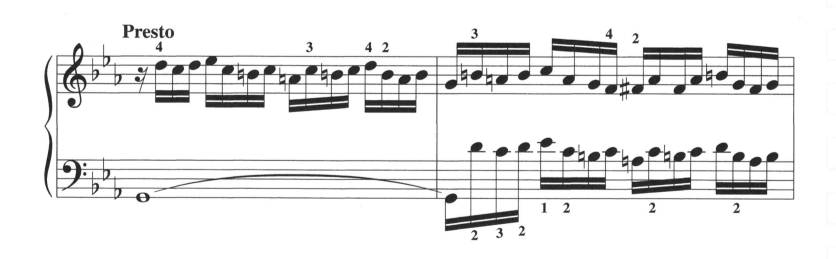

Fugue

Air
from Suite in D Major

Johann Sebastian Bach (1685–1750)

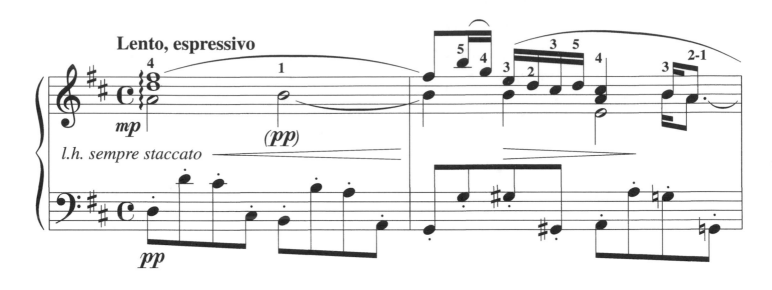

Bagatelle

Op. 126, No. 5

Ludwig van Beethoven (1770–1817)

Quasi allegretto

Ecossaise

Ludwig van Beethoven (1770–1817)

Leggero ed animato

marcato

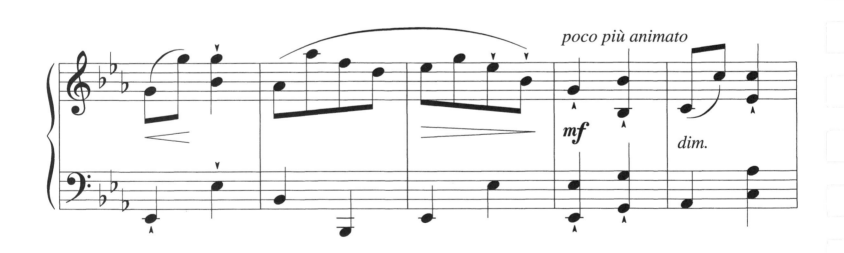

Für Elise

Ludwig van Beethoven (1770–1817)

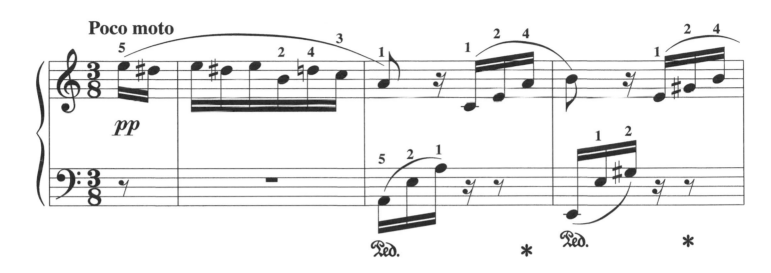

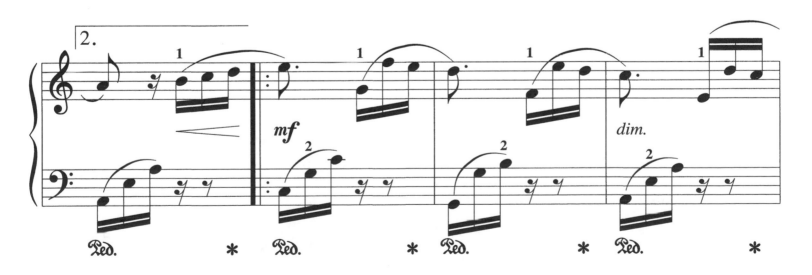

Minuet in G

Ludwig van Beethoven (1770–1817)

Allegretto (♩ = 120)

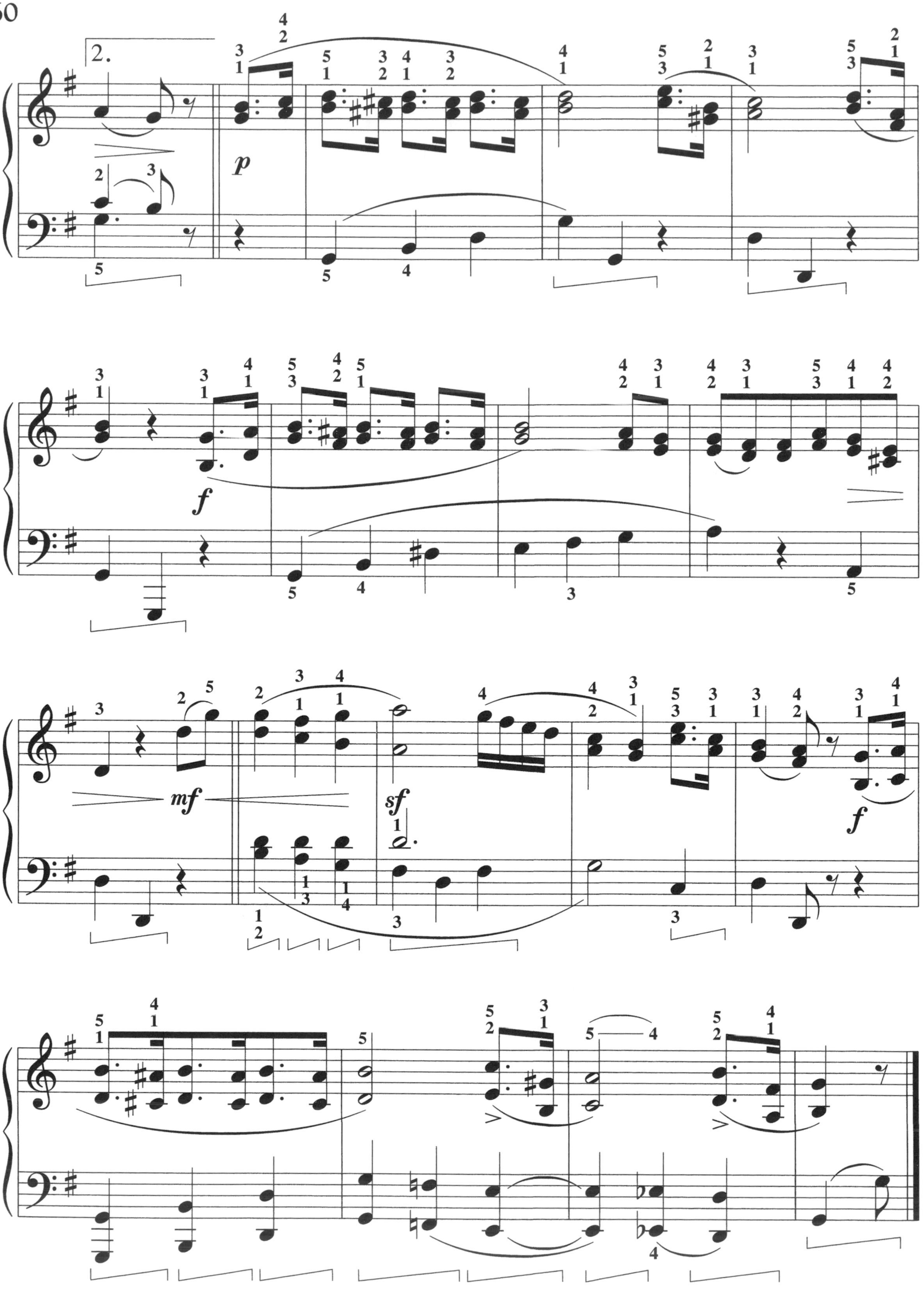
2.
p
f
mf
sf
f

Moonlight Sonata

First Movement, Op. 27, No. 2

Ludwig van Beethoven (1770–1817)

Adagio sostenuto

sempre **pp**

una corda

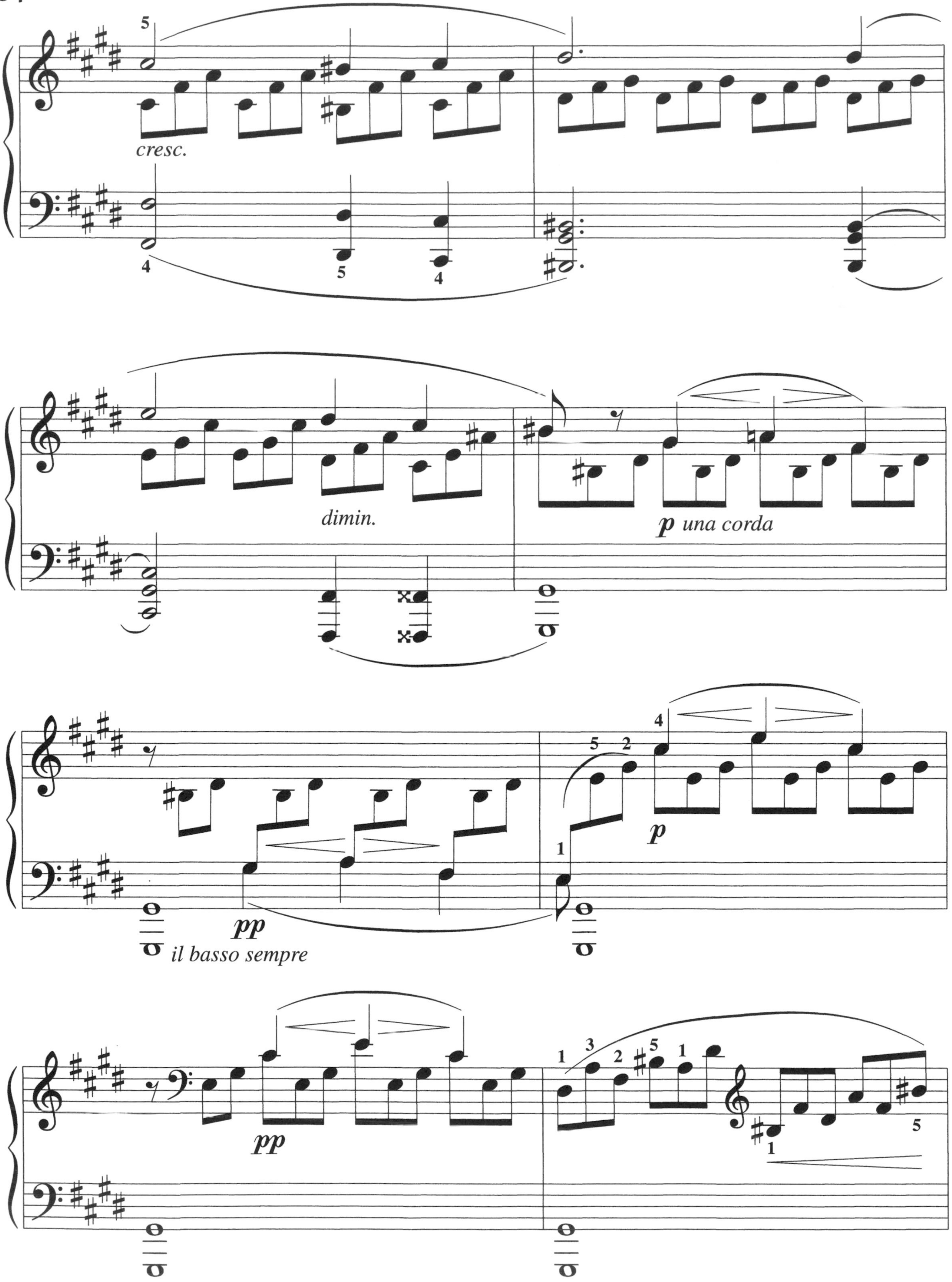
cresc.
dimin.
p una corda
pp
il basso sempre
p
pp

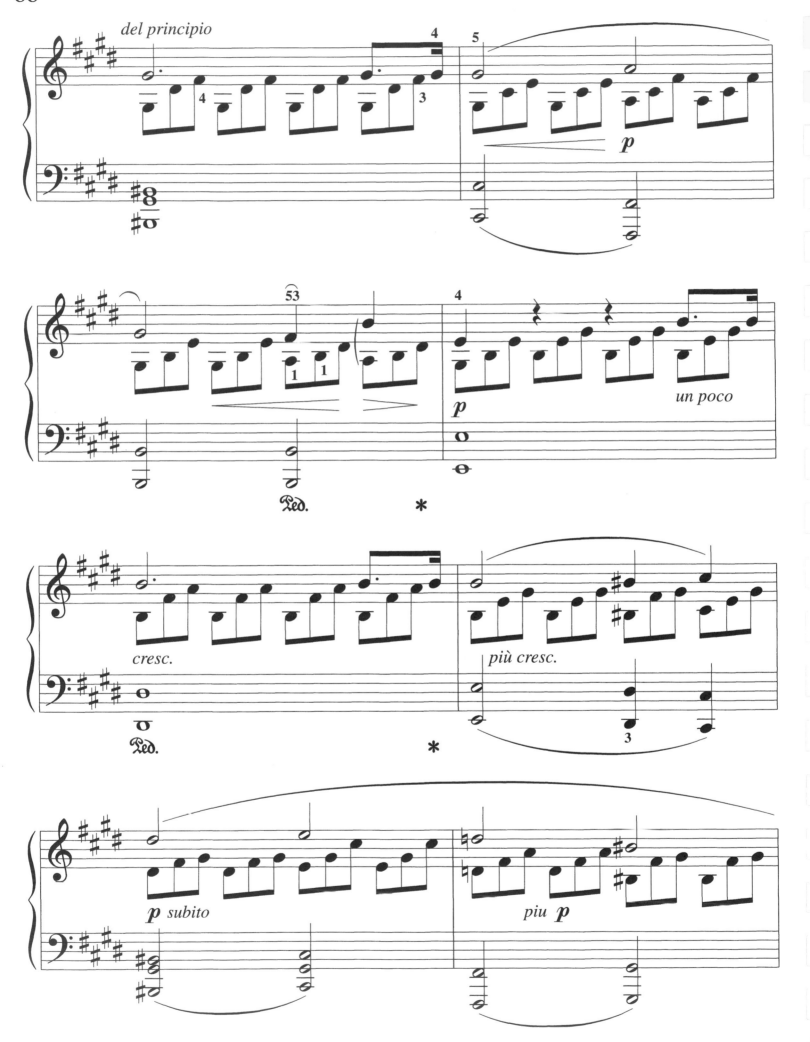

Minuet

Luigi Boccherini (1743–1805)

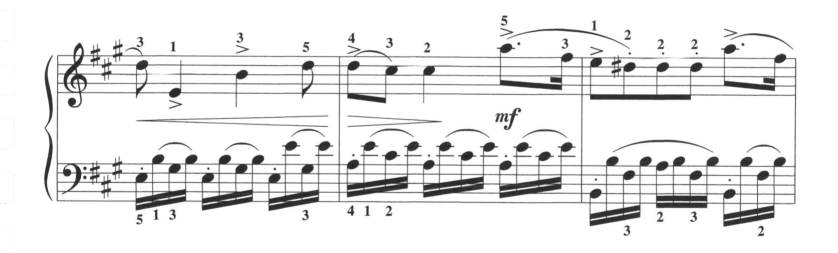

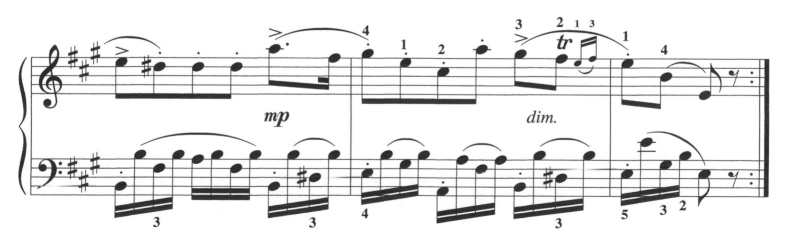

Waltz in A-Flat
Op. 39, No. 15

Johannes Brahms (1833–1897)

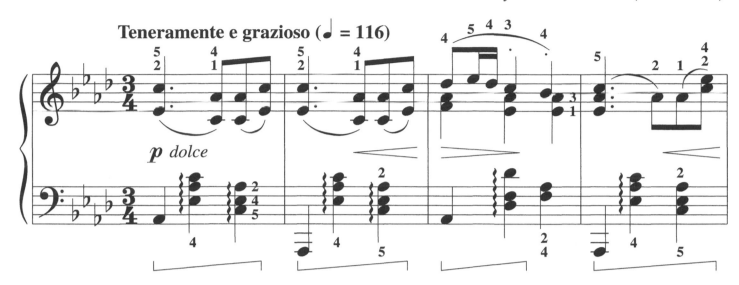

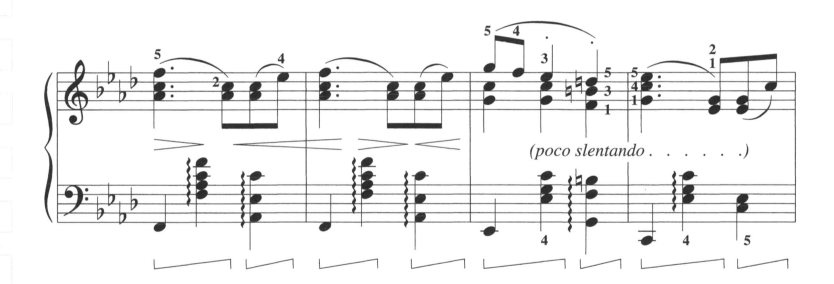

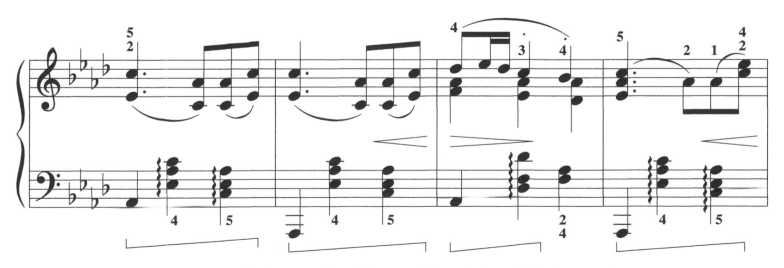

(poco slentando . . . . .)

(poco largamente . .

poco cresc.

. . . .)

f

p

(poco ritenuto

Hungarian Dance
No. 5

Johannes Brahms (1833–1897)

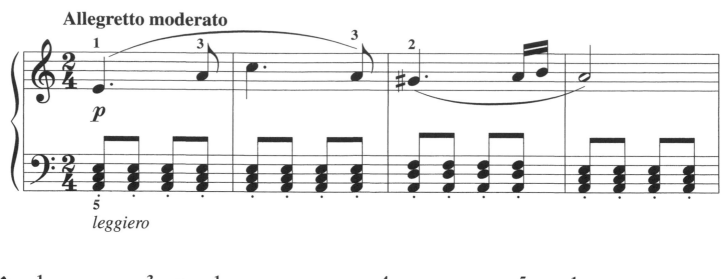

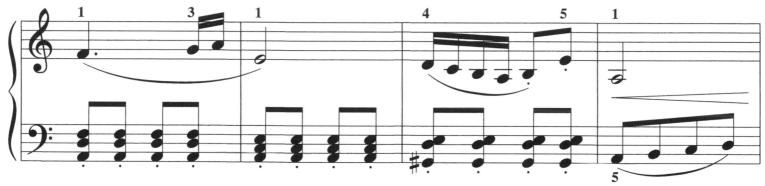

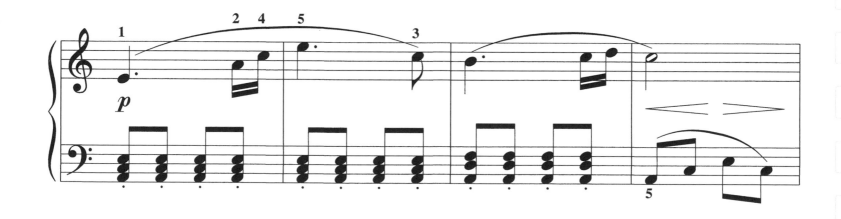

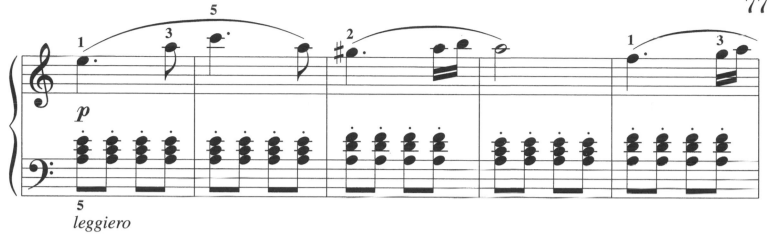

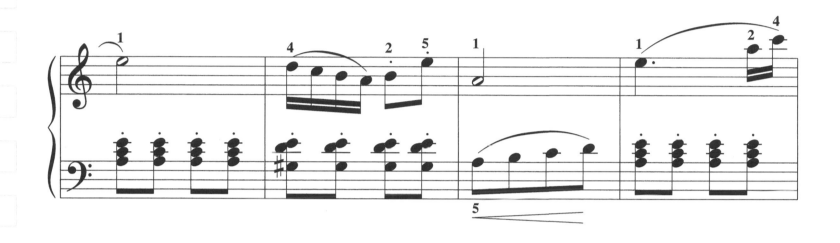

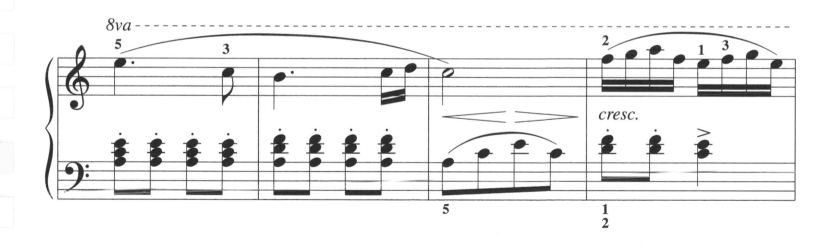

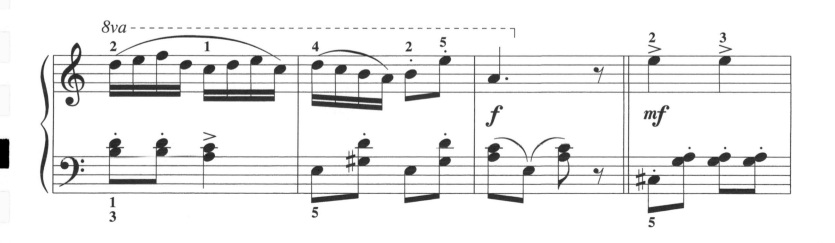

Prelude

Op. 28, No. 6

Frédéric Chopin (1810–1849)

Prelude
Op. 28, No. 7

Frédéric Chopin (1810–1849)

Valse

Op. 69, No. 2

Frédéric Chopin (1810–1849)

84

Mazurka in B-Flat

Op. 7, No. 1

Frédéric Chopin (1810–1849)

Valse

Op. 64, No. 1

Frédéric Chopin (1810–1849)

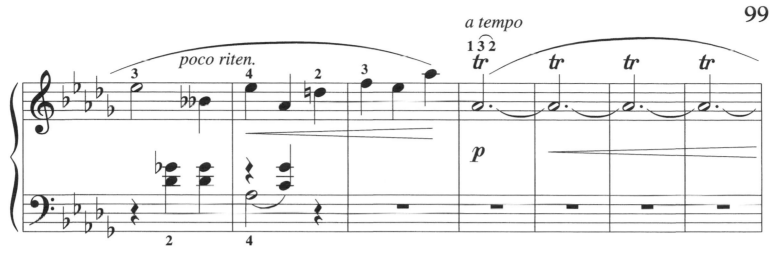

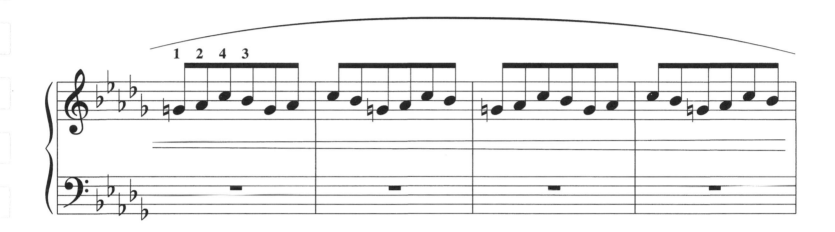

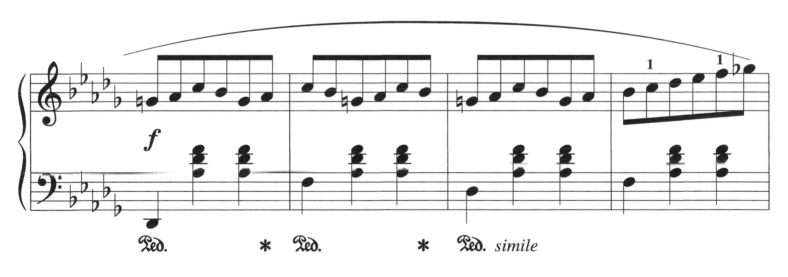

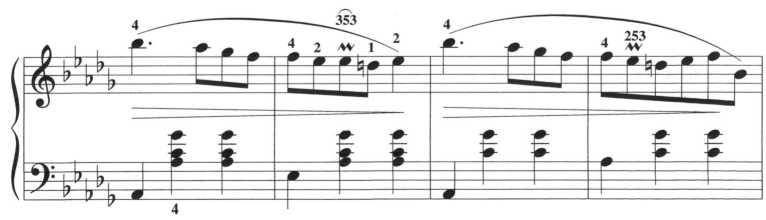

Clair de Lune

Claude Debussy (1862–1918)

Andante très expressif

pp   *con sordina*

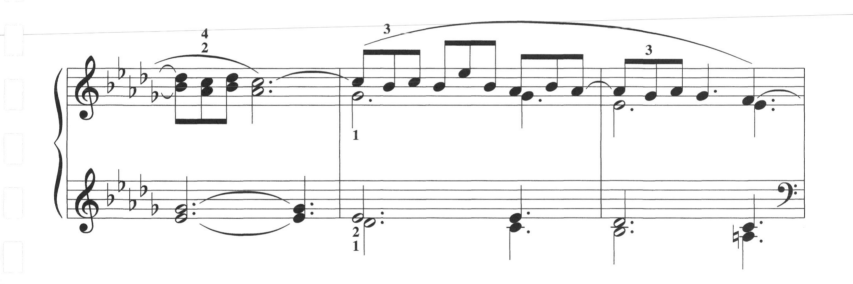

morendo jusqu'à la fin

Humoresque
Op. 101, No. 7

Antonín Dvořák (1841–1904)

Poco lento e grazioso (♩ = 72)

p leggiero

senza

senza

p

dim.

pp

mf

f

dim.

Rondino

Antonio Diabelli (1781–1858)

Poem

Zdeněk Fibich (1850–1900)

Slowly, with expression

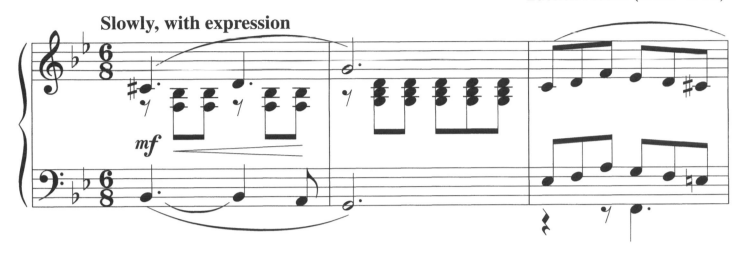

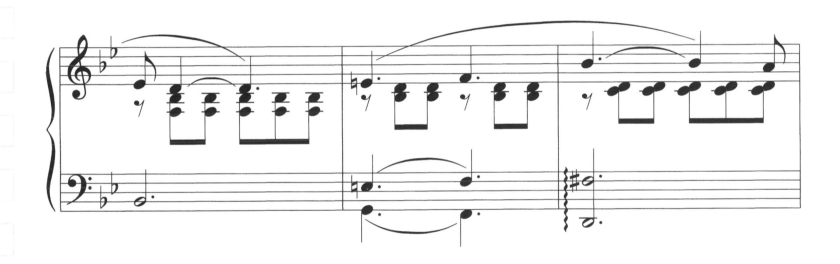

Anitra's Dance

from Peer Gynt

Edvard Grieg (1843–1907)

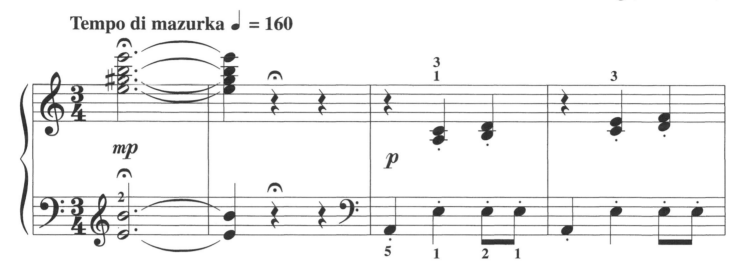

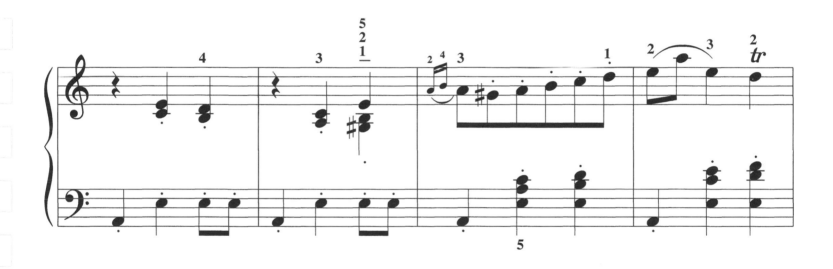

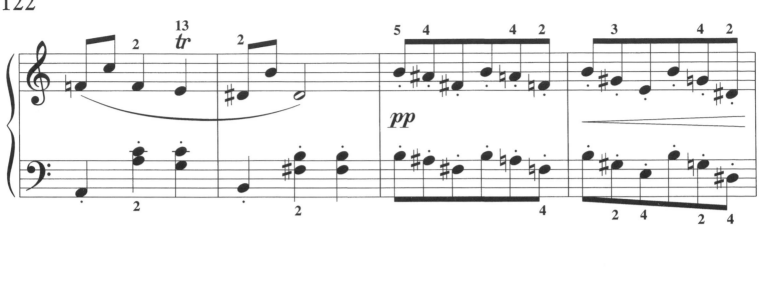

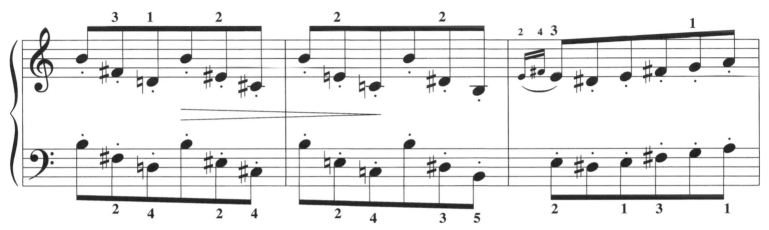

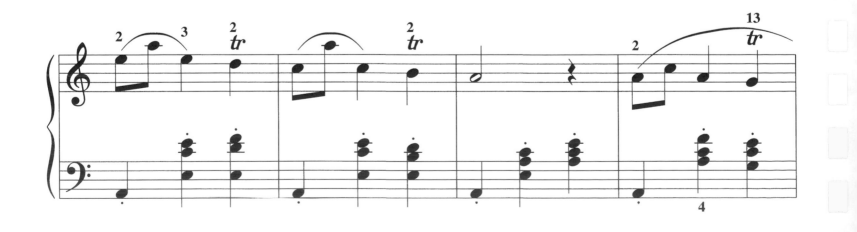

Gavotte in D

François Joseph Gossec (1734–1829)

Poco allegro ma non troppo

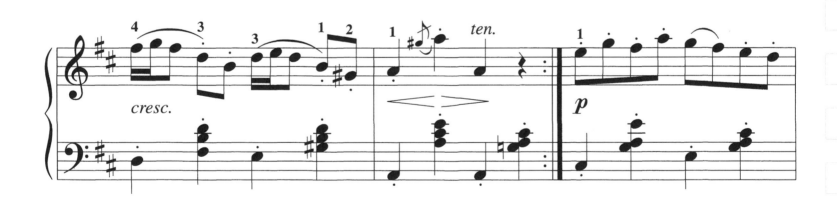

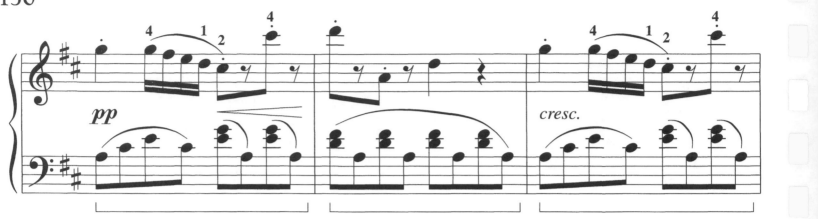

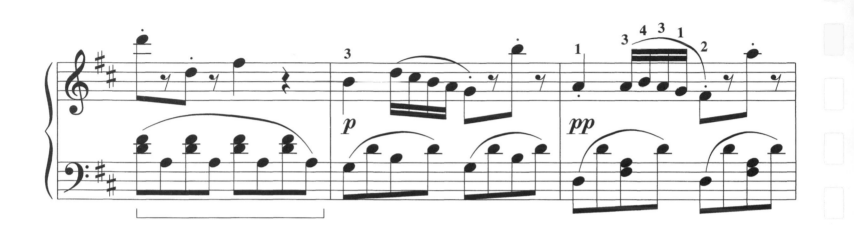

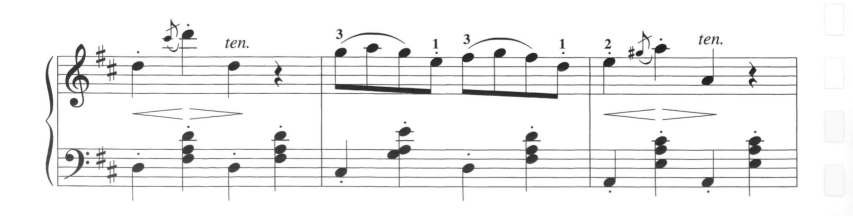

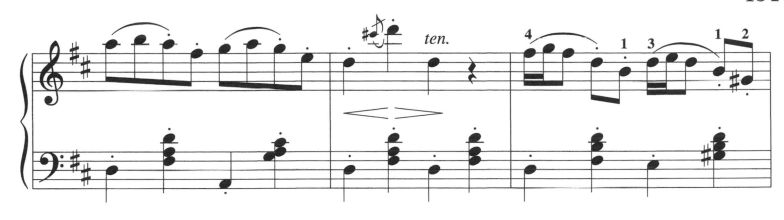

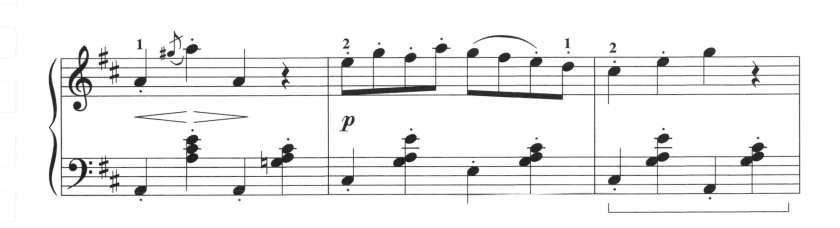

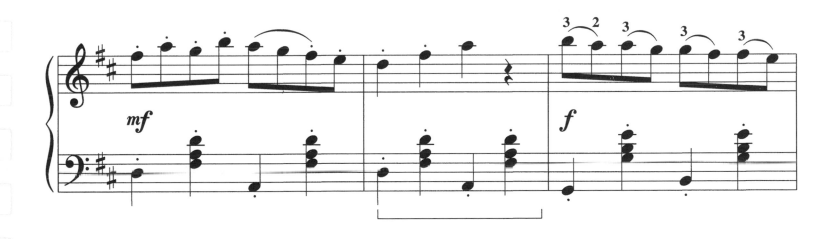

Largo

George Frideric Handel (1685–1759)

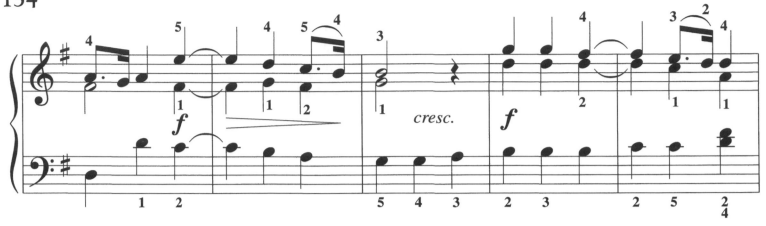

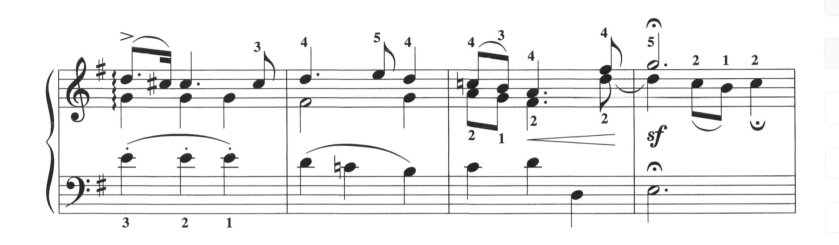

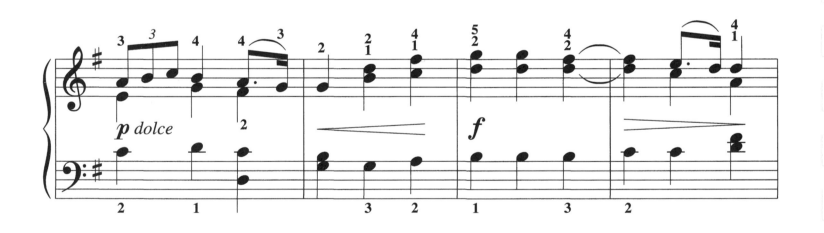

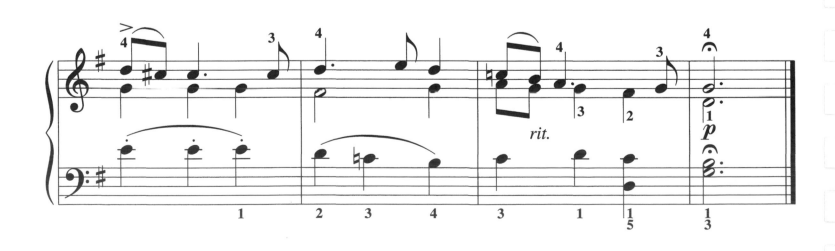

Gypsy Rondo

Joseph Haydn (1732–1809)

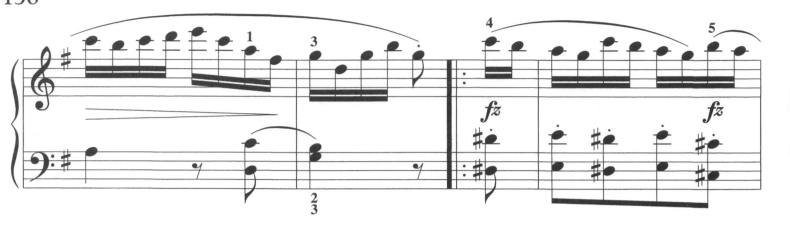

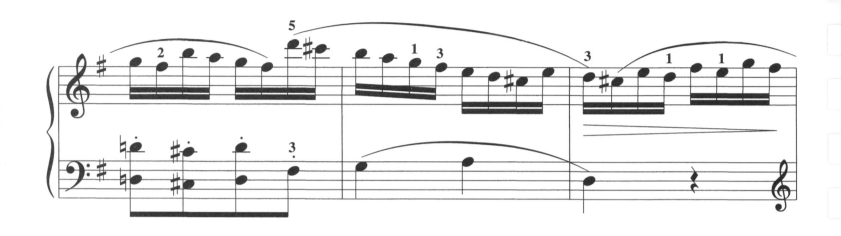

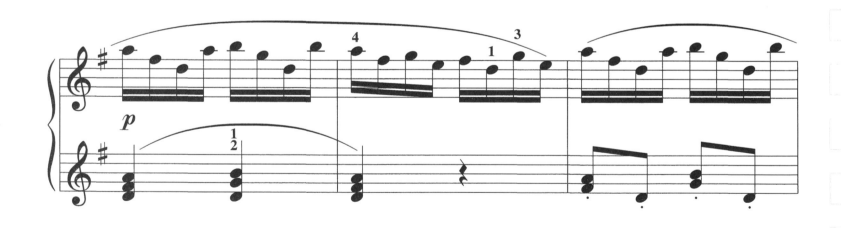

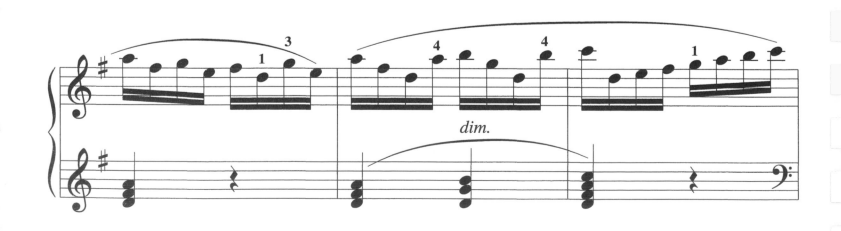

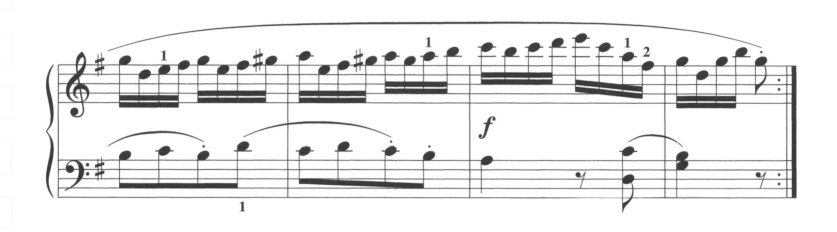

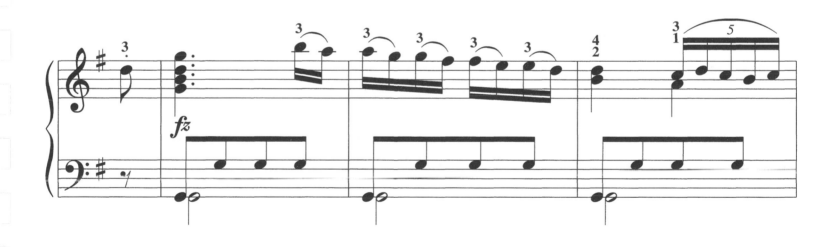

Minore I

Maggiore

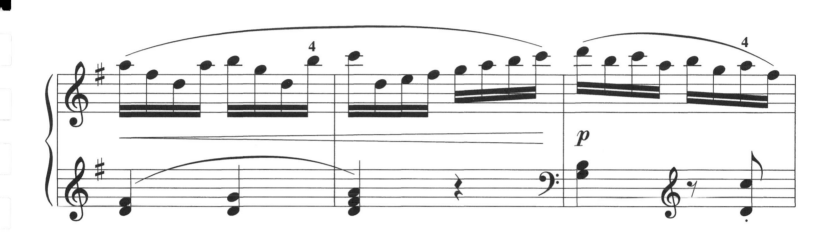

Minore II

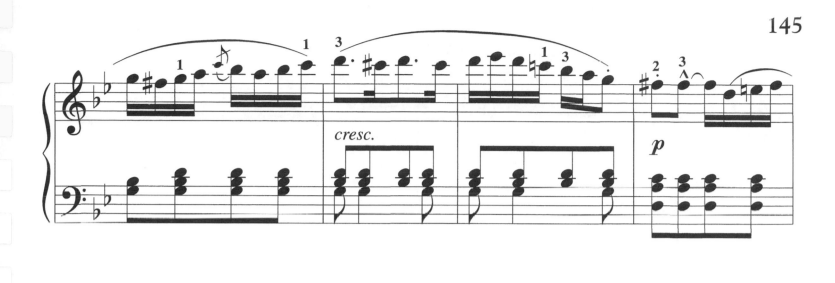

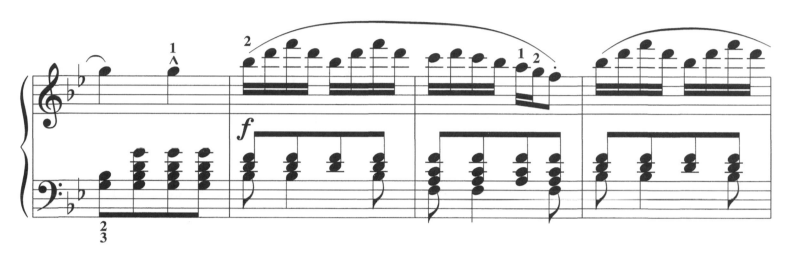

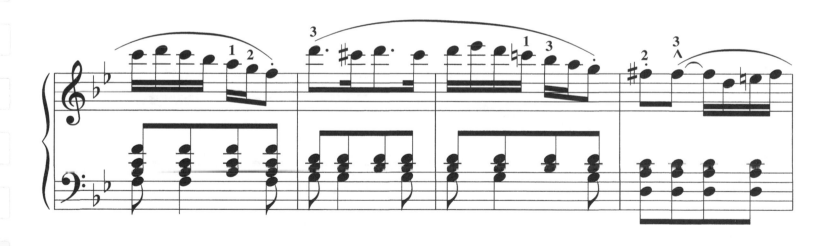

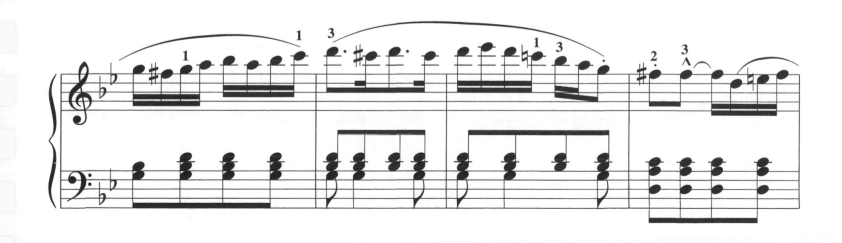

Maggiore

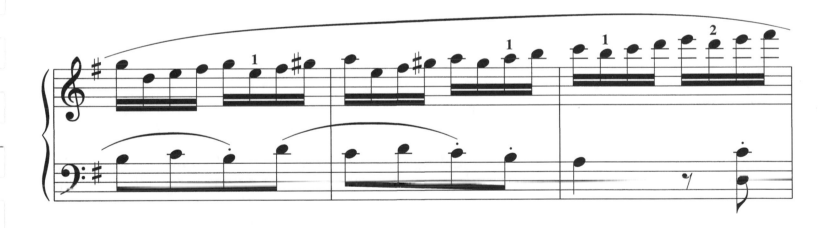

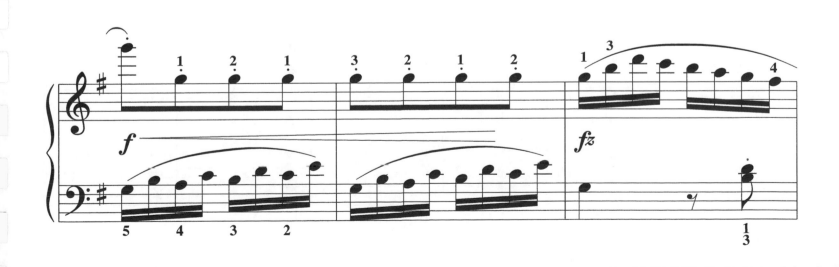

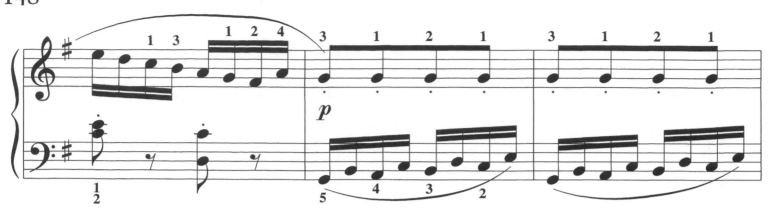

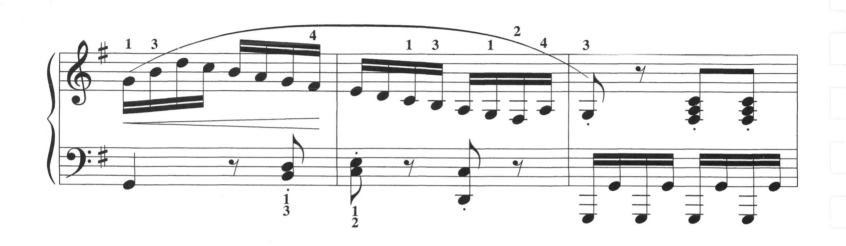

The Cascades

Scott Joplin (1868–1919)

Tempo di Marcia

152

Liebestraum

Notturno No. 3

Franz Liszt (1811–1886)

Poco allegro, con affetto

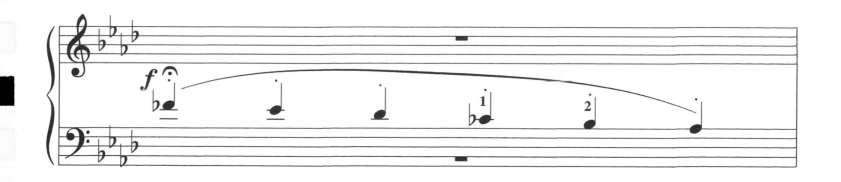

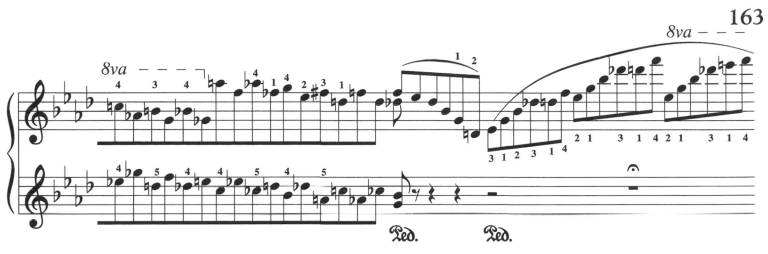

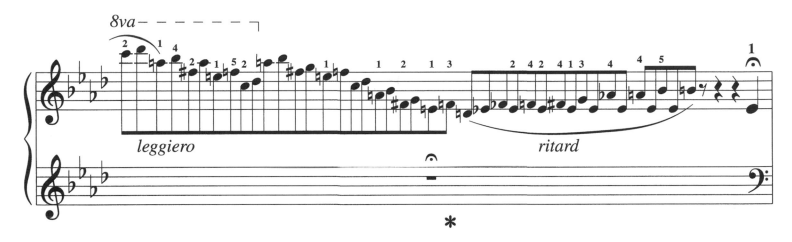

Tempo primo

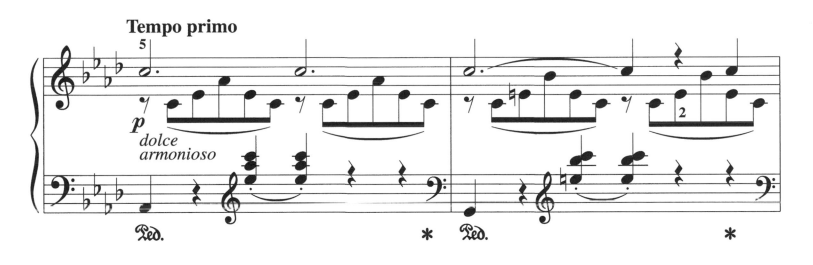

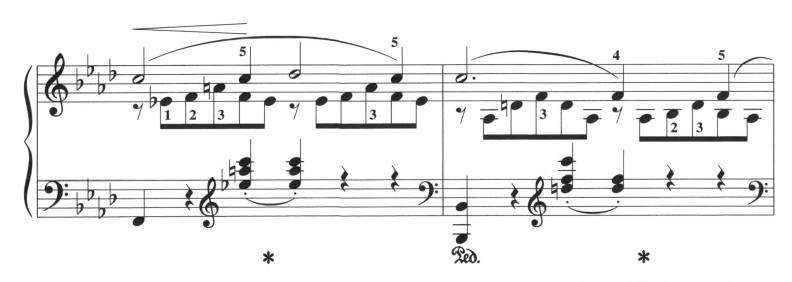

To a Wild Rose

Op. 51, No. 1

Edward MacDowell (1861–1908)

Elegie
Melodie Op. 10

Jules Massenet (1842–1912)

Lento, ma non troppo

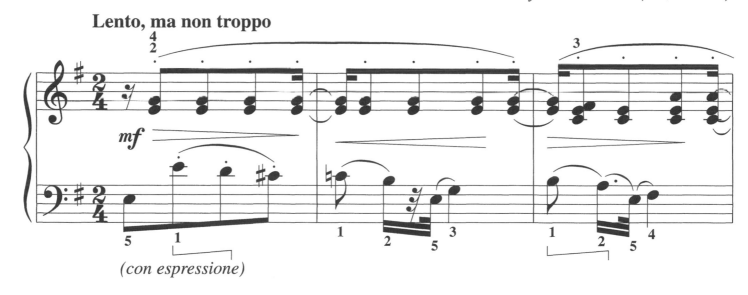

(con espressione)

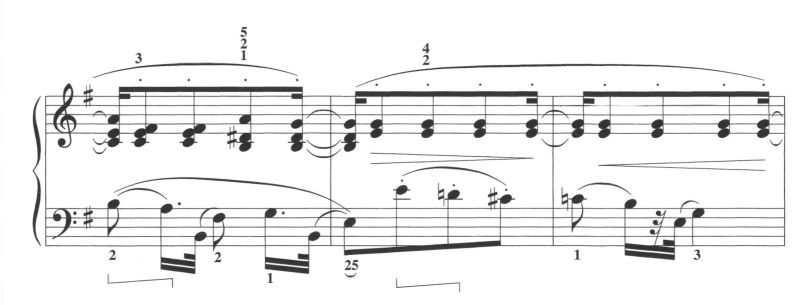

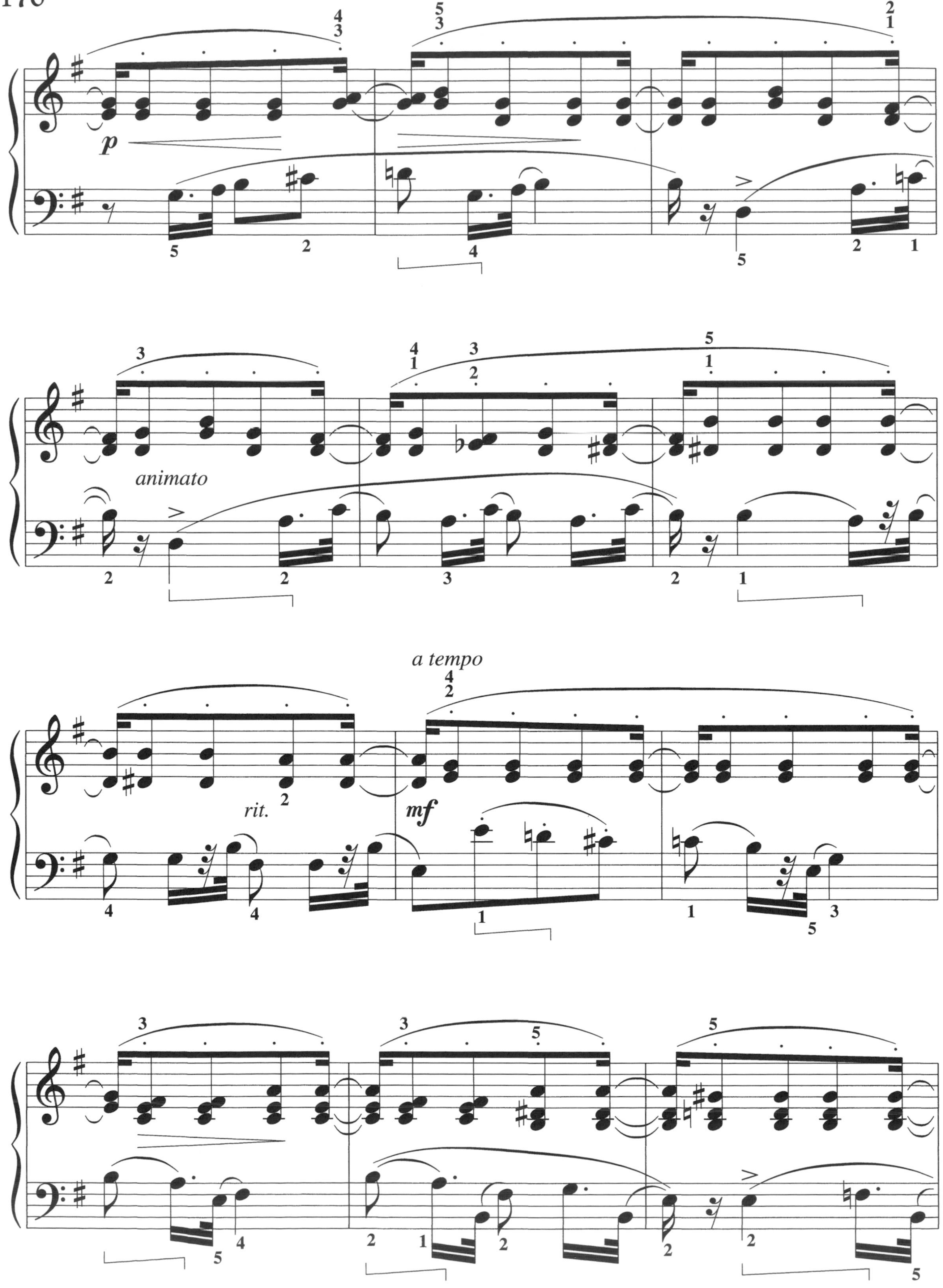
p
animato
a tempo
rit.
mf

Venetian Boat Song

Op. 19, No. 6

Felix Mendelssohn (1809–1847)

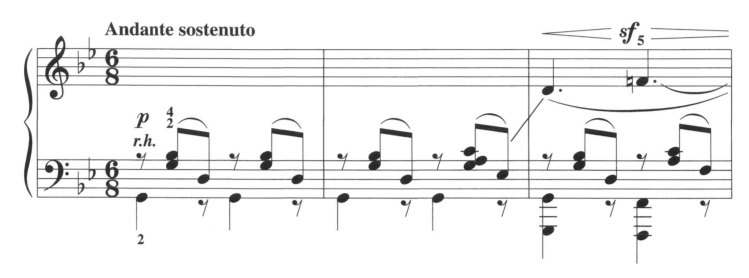

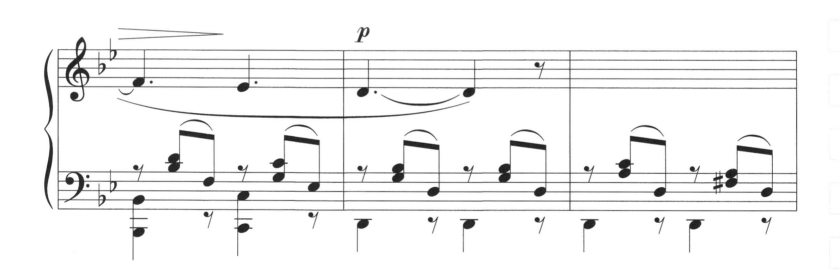

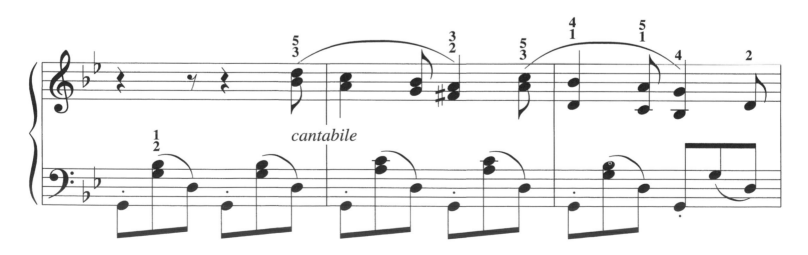

Alla Turca

From Sonata K. 331

Wolfgang Amadeus Mozart (1756–1791)

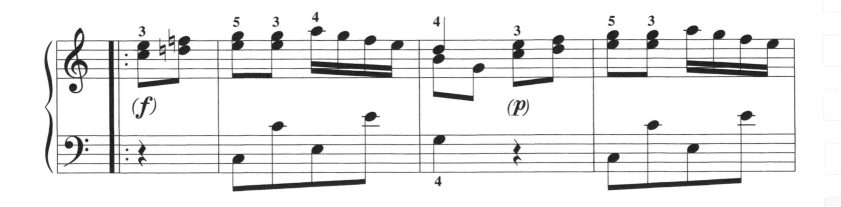

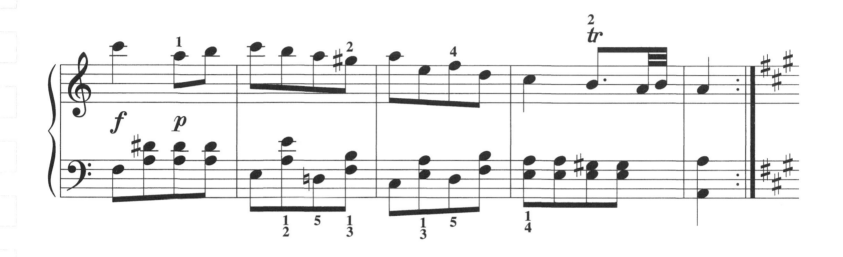

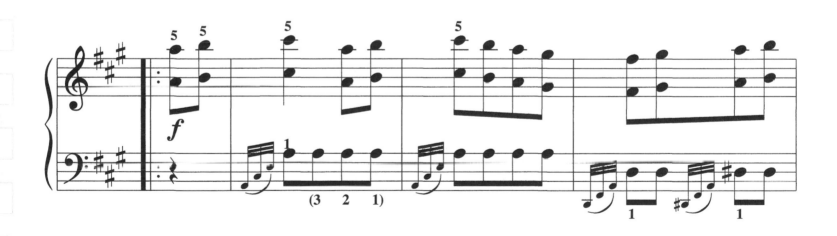

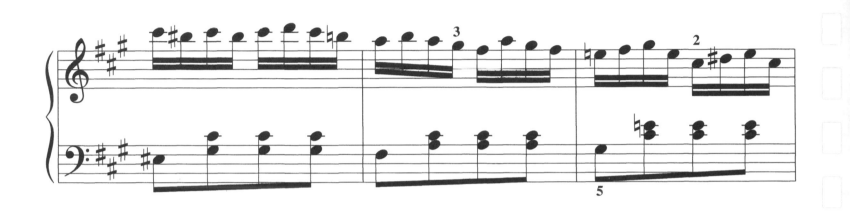

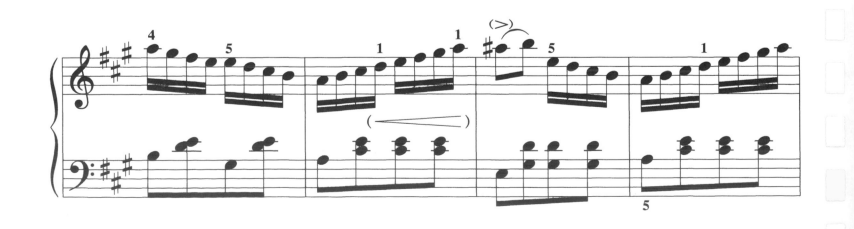

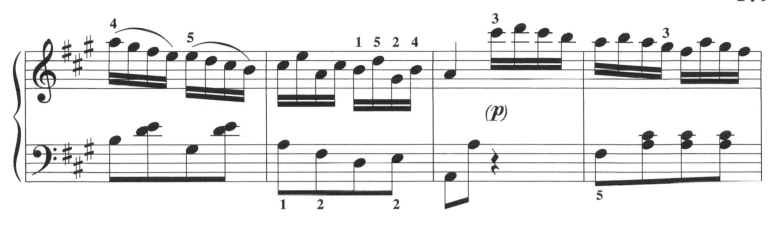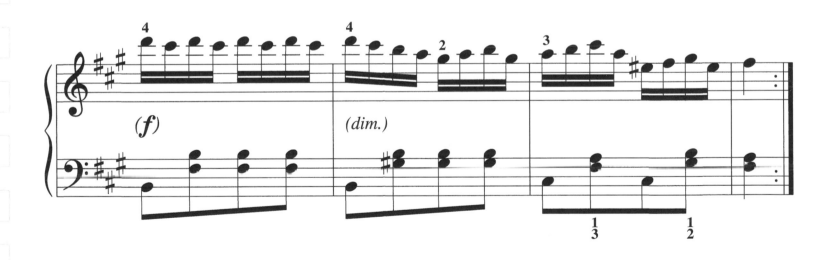

Sonata

First Movement, K. 331

Wolfgang Amadeus Mozart (1756–1791)

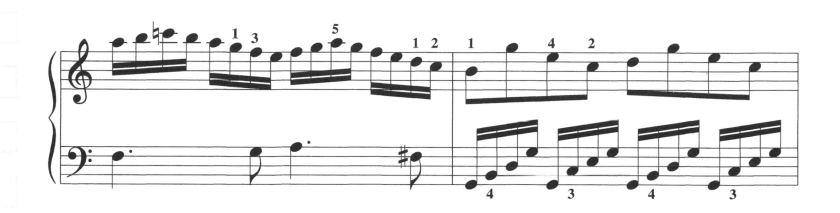

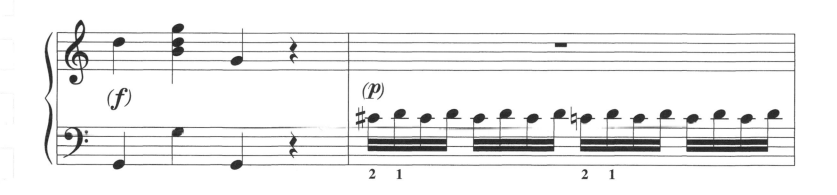

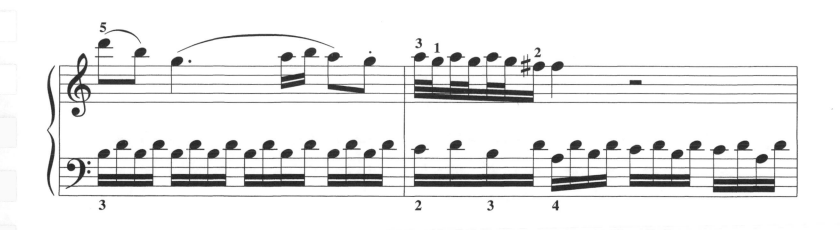

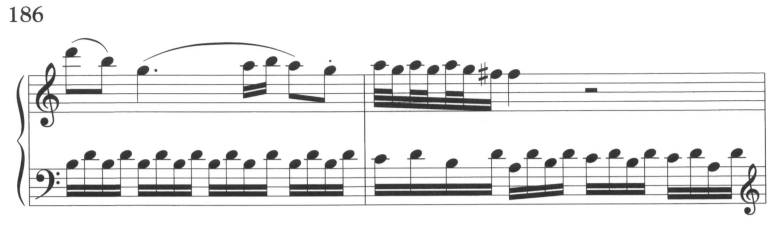

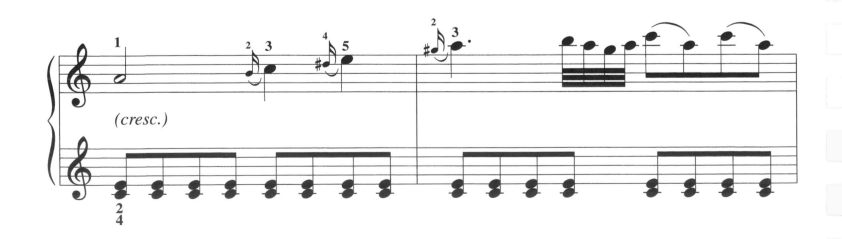

(cresc.)

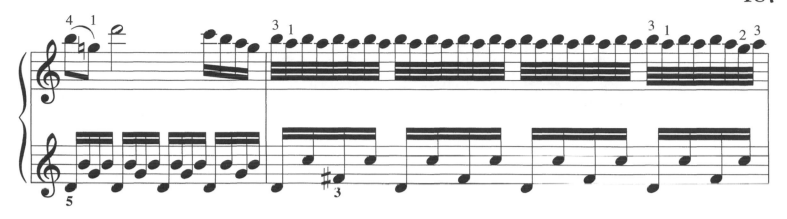

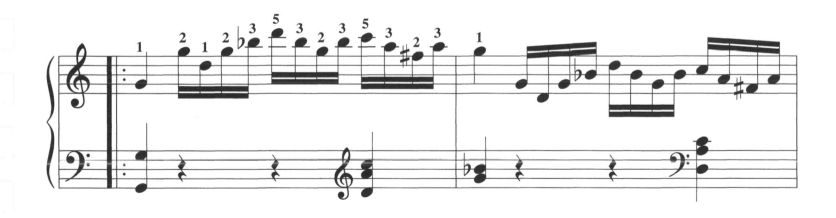

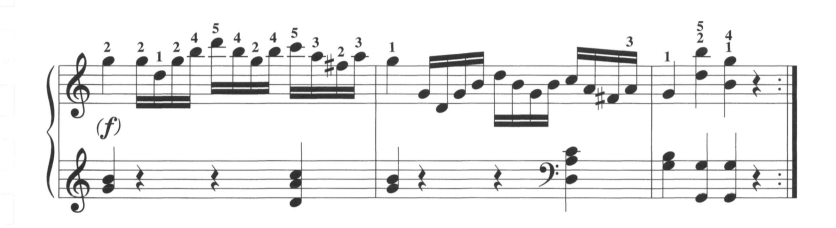

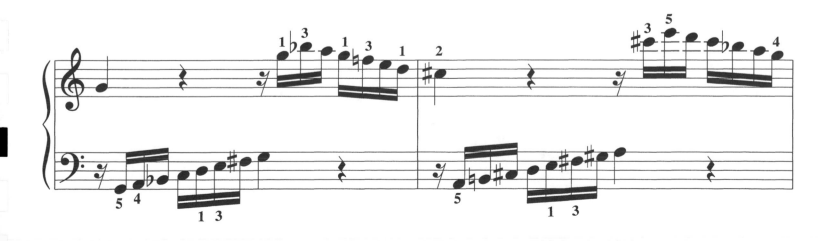

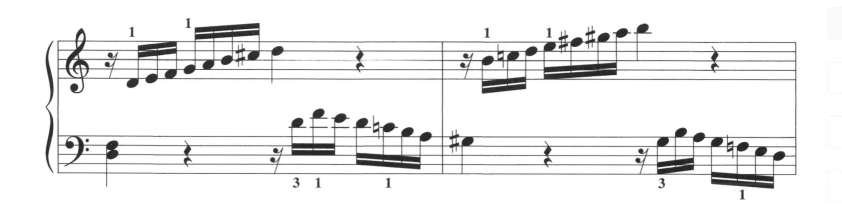

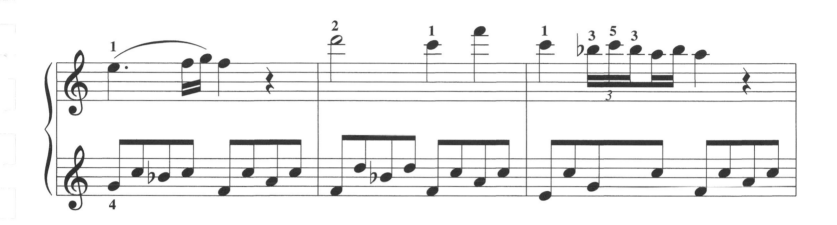

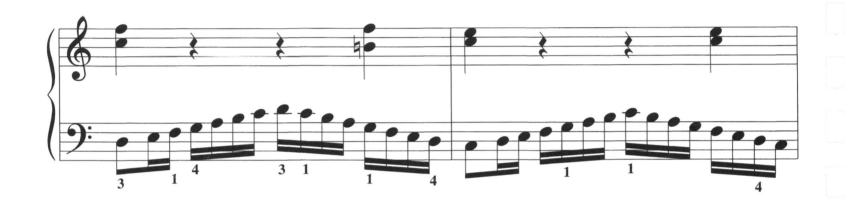

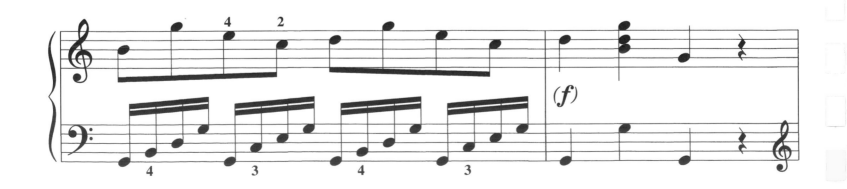

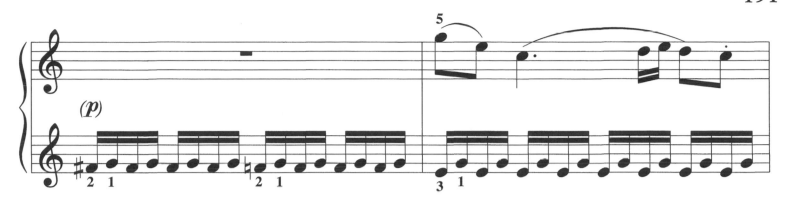

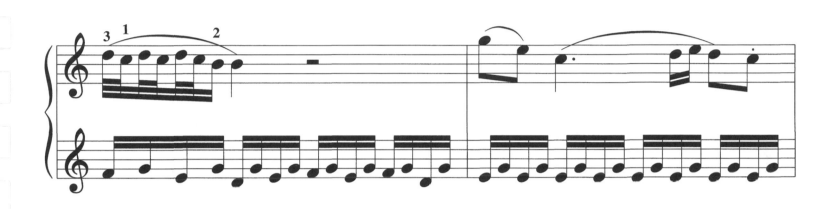

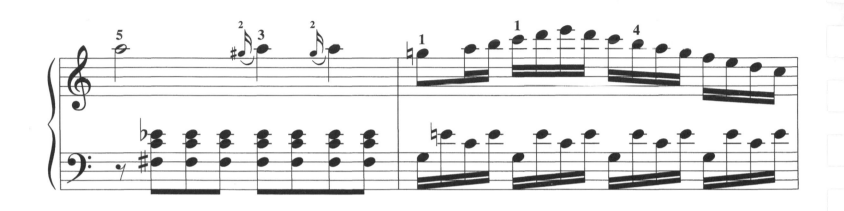

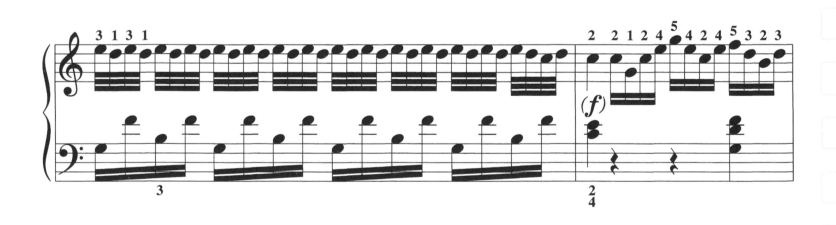

Rondo in D
K. 485

Wolfgang Amadeus Mozart (1756–1791)

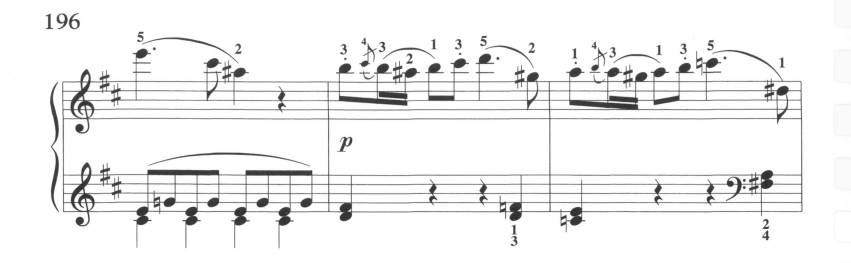

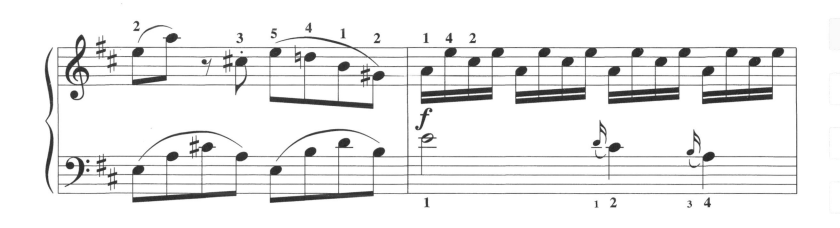

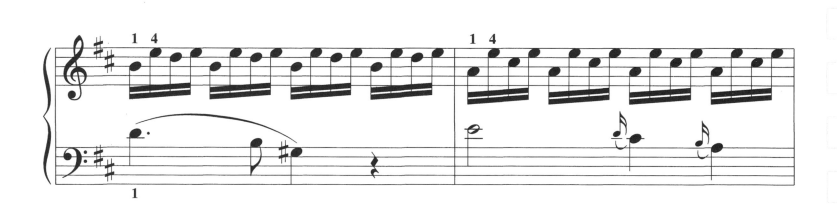

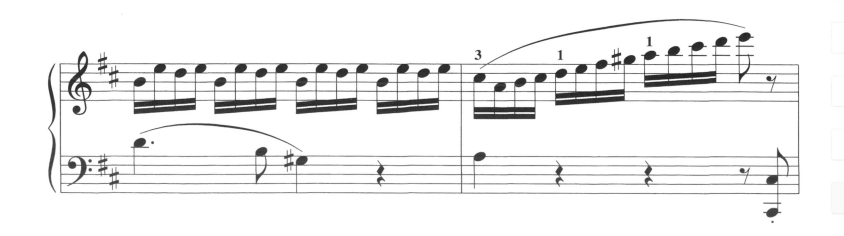

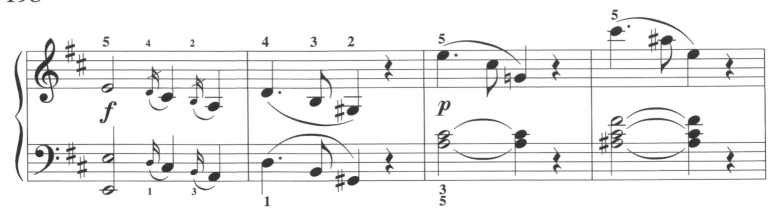

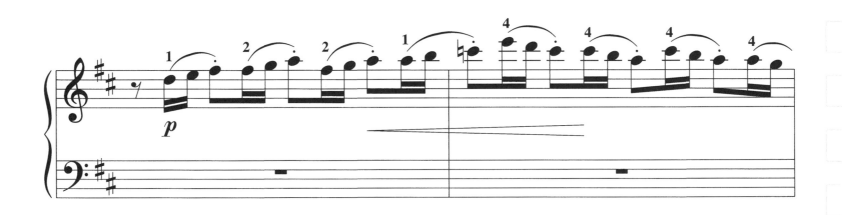

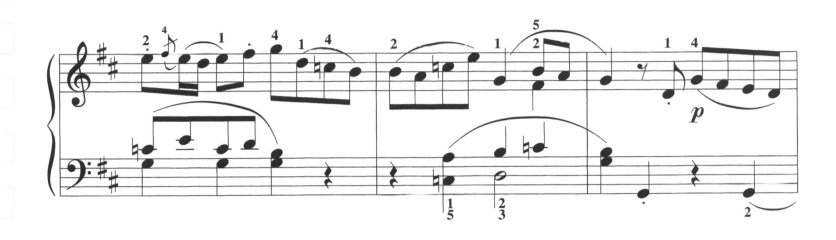

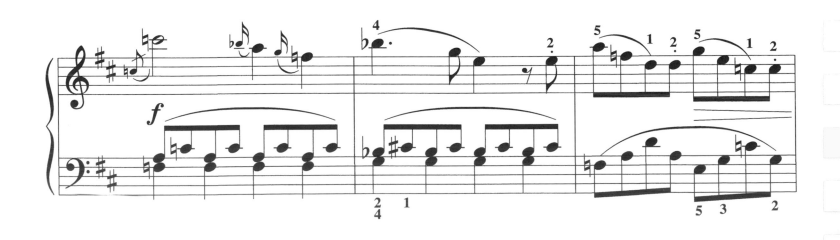

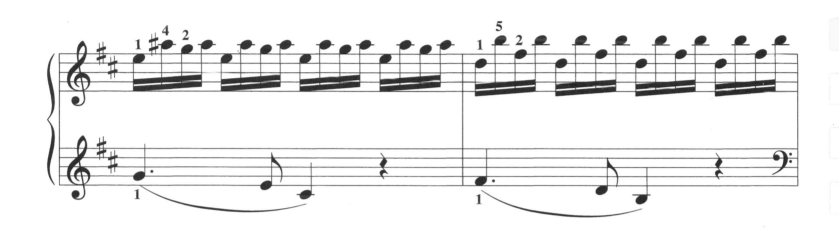

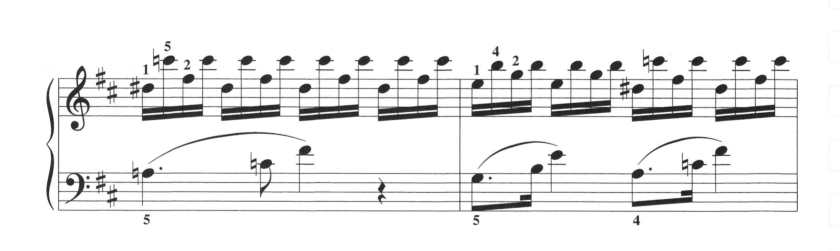

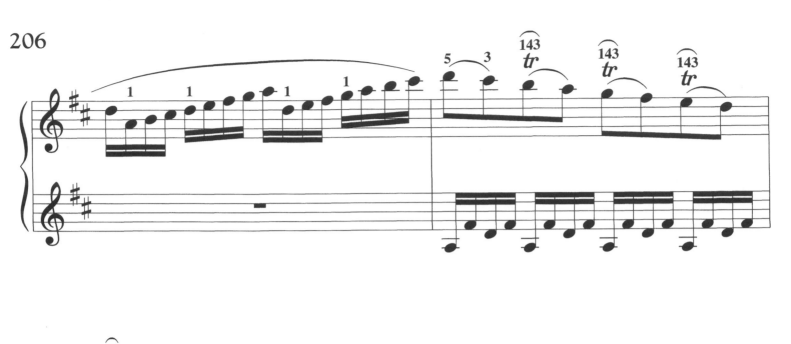

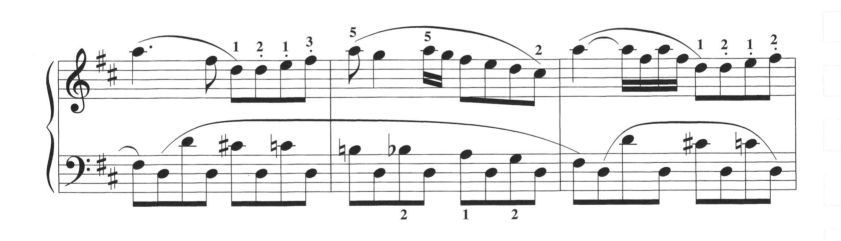

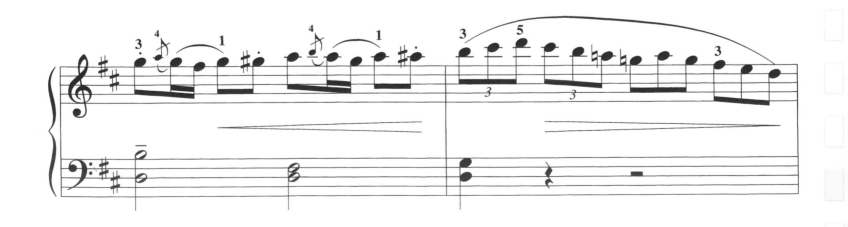

Barcarolle

From Tales of Hoffman

Jacques Offenbach (1819–1880)

La Tambourin

Jean-Philippe Rameau (1683–1764)

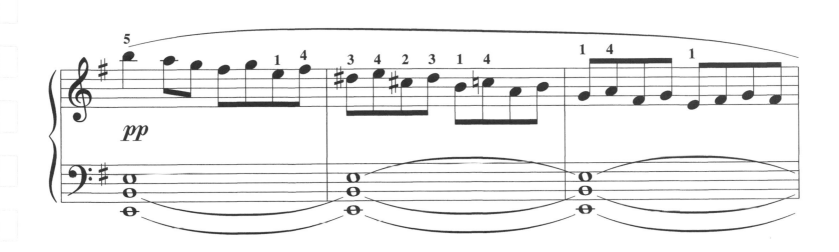

Song of India

Nikolai Rimsky-Korsakov (1844–1908)

Sonata
L. 375

Domenico Scarlatti (1685–1757)

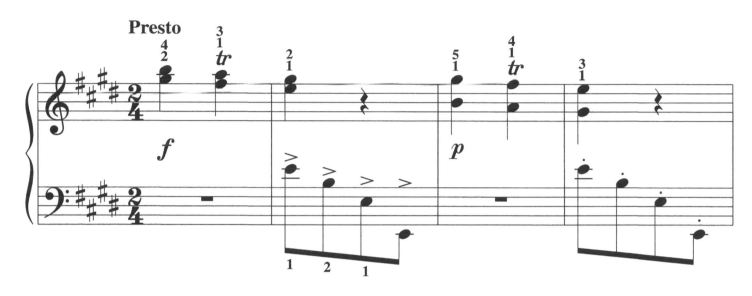

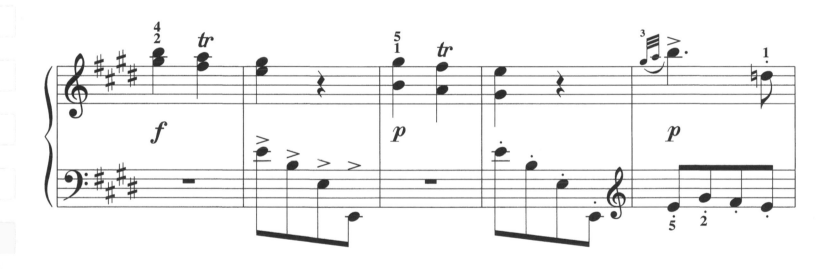

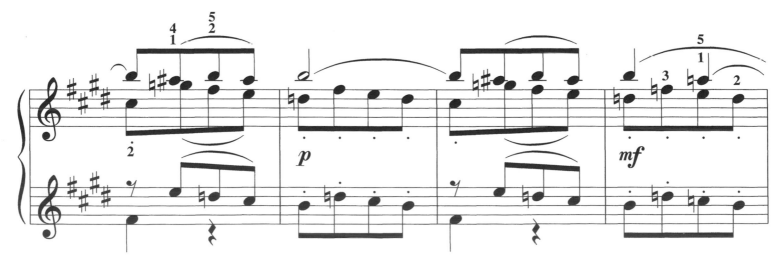

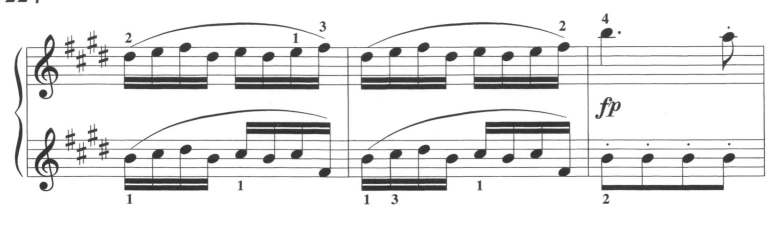

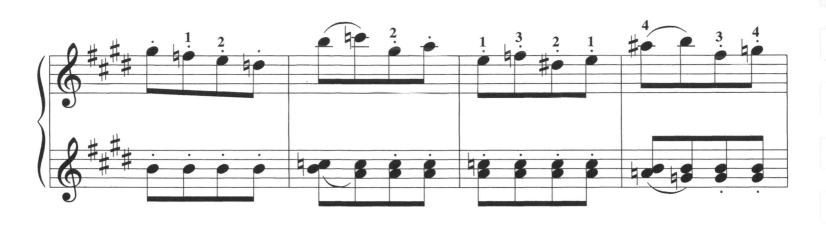

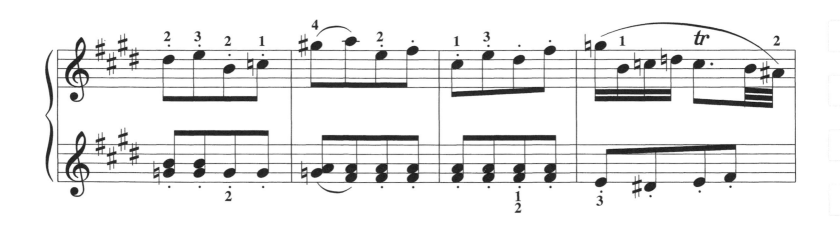

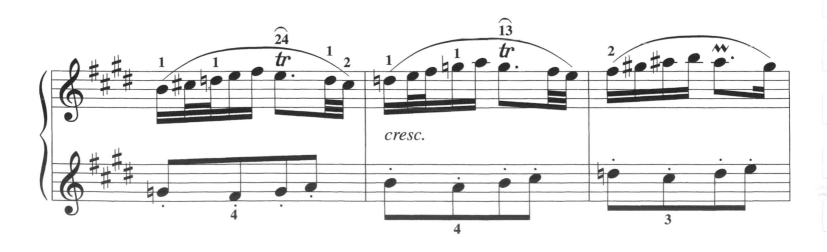

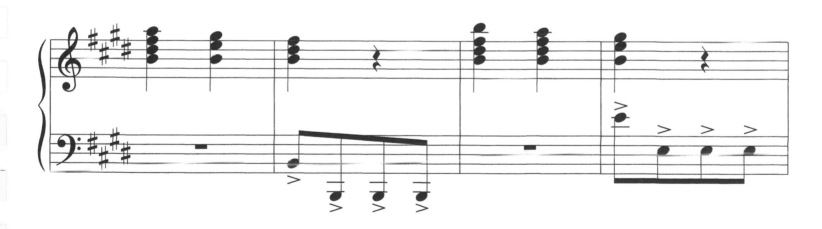

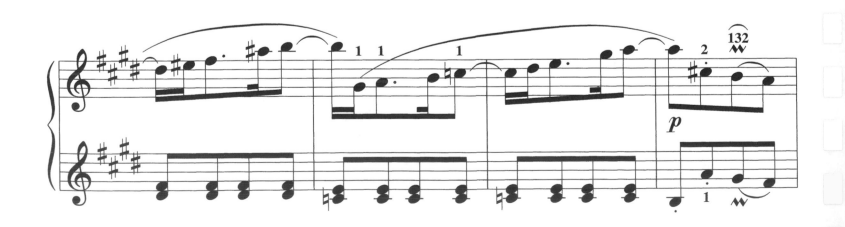

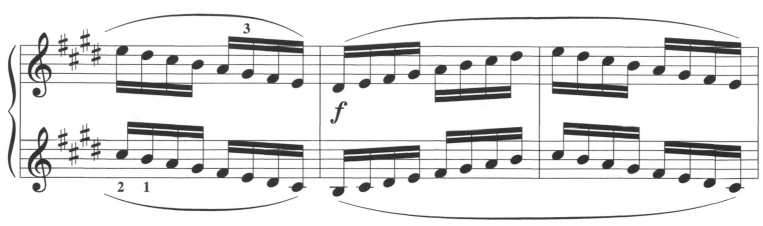

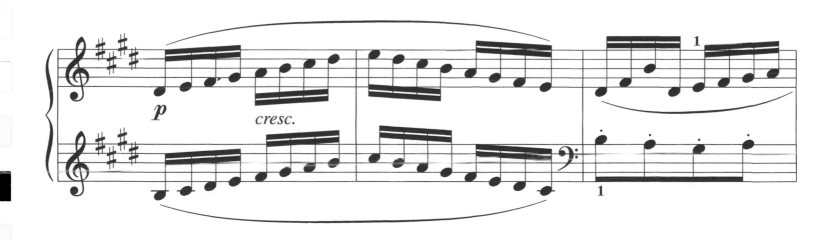

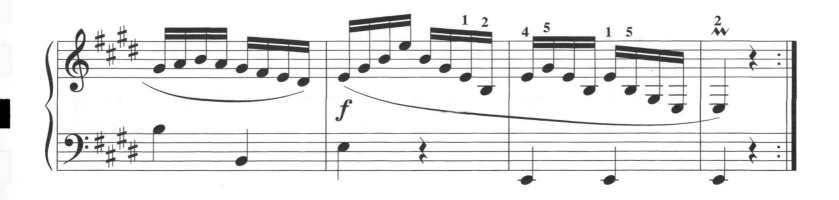

Italian Song

Op. 39, No. 15

Peter Ilyich Tchaikovsky (1840–1893)

Serenade

Franz Schubert (1797–1828)

Moment Musical
Op. 94, No. 3

Franz Schubert (1797–1828)

Allegro moderato

(staccato sempre)

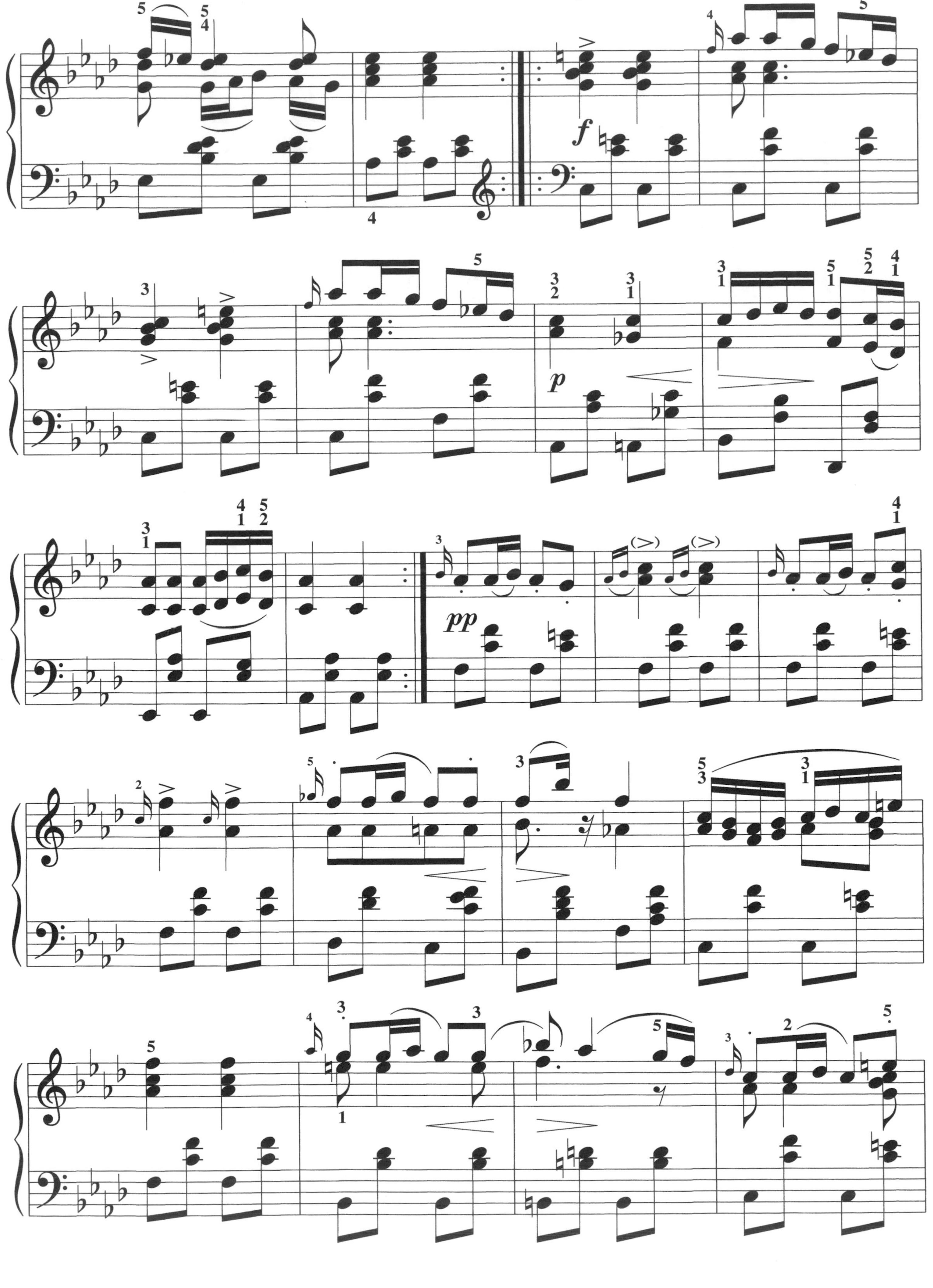
f
p
pp

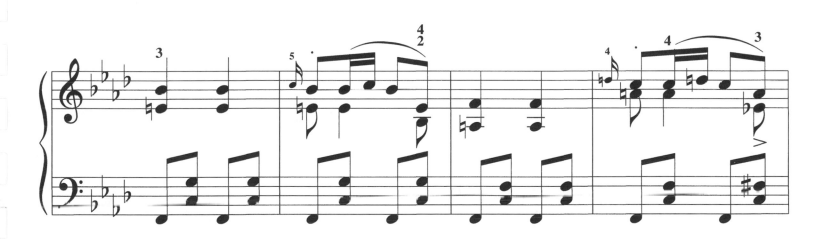

Soldiers' March

From Album for the Young

Robert Schumann (1810–1856)

Munter und staff *(happy but strict)*

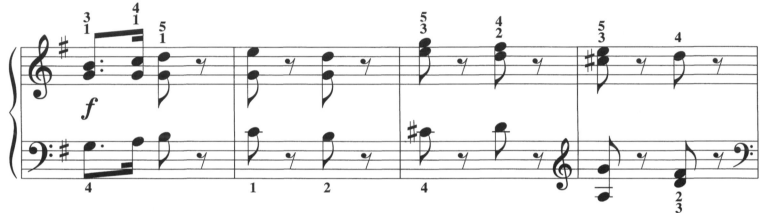

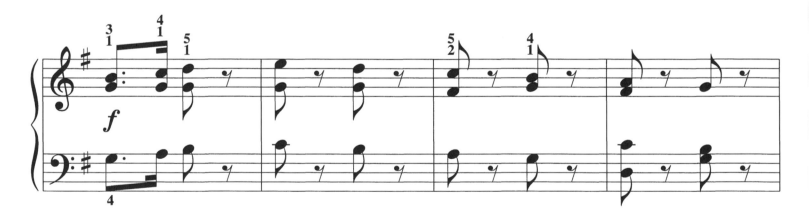

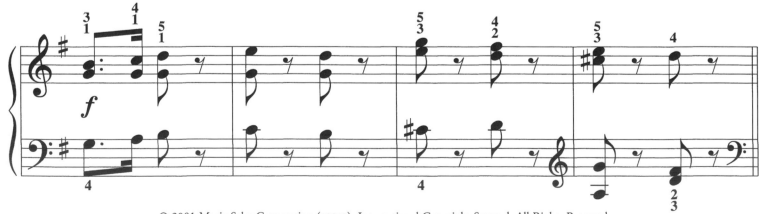

Marche Militaire

Op. 51, No. 1

Franz Schubert (1797–1828)

Marcia D.C. al Fine

The Happy Farmer

From Album for the Young

Robert Schumann (1810–1856)

Frisch und munter *(bright and happy)*

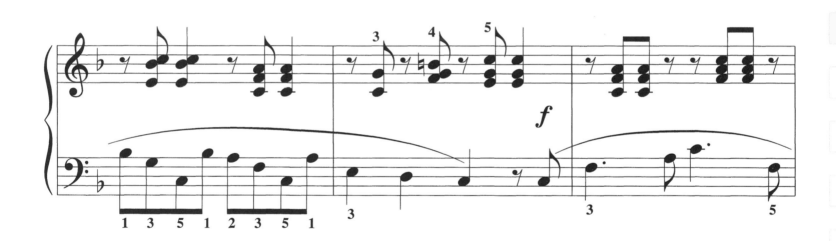

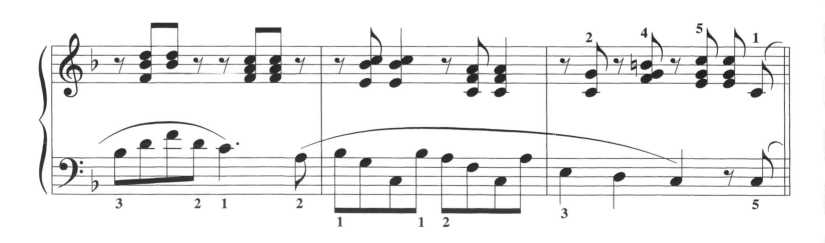

Träumerei

Robert Schumann (1810–1856)

The Beautiful Blue Danube

Johann Strauss (1825–1899)

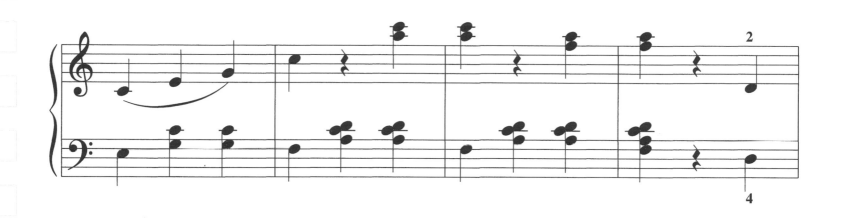

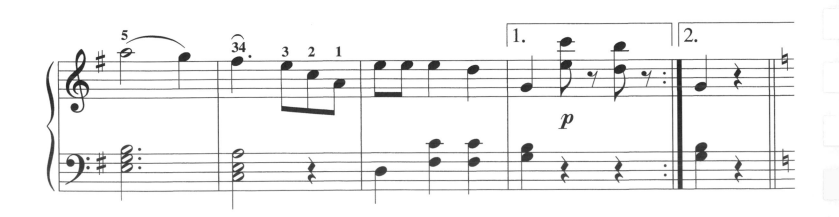

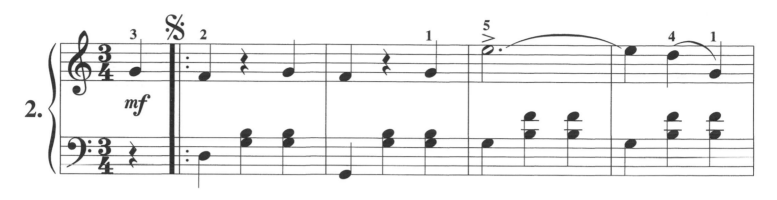

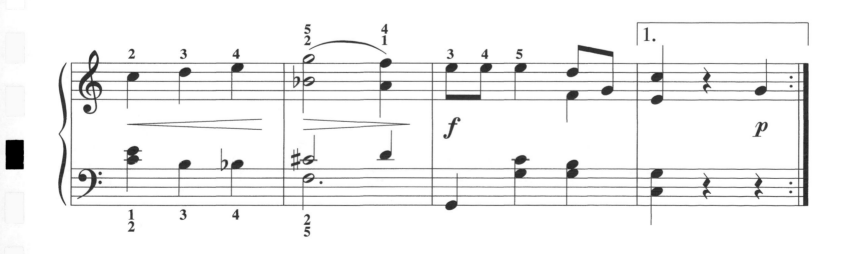

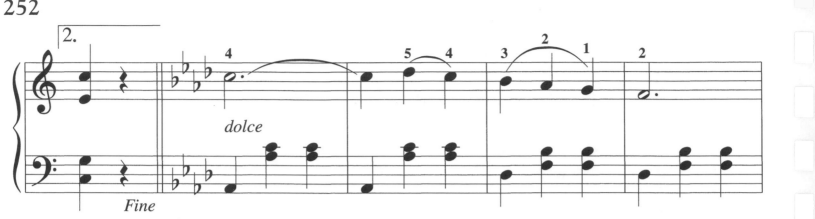

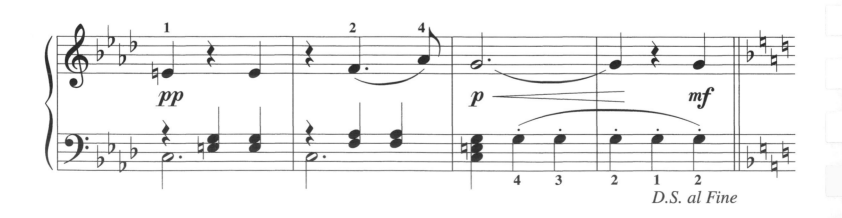

Waltz

Carl Maria von Weber (1786–1826)

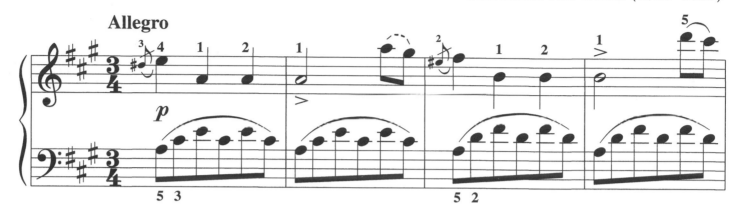

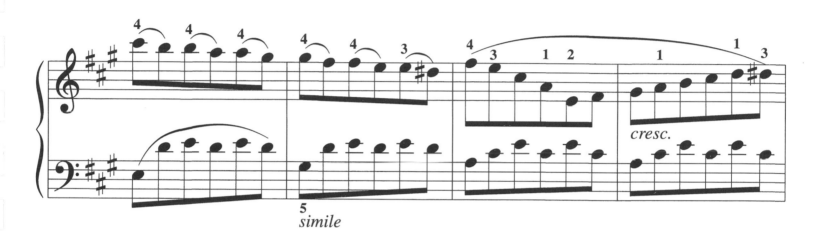

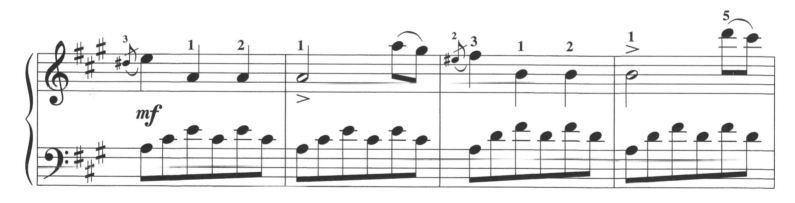

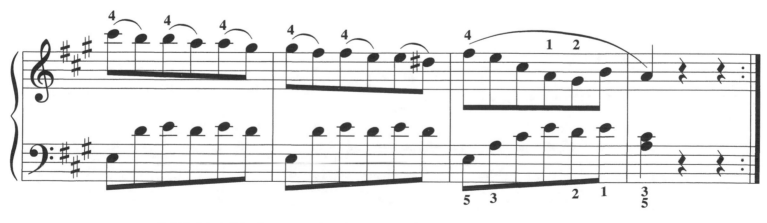

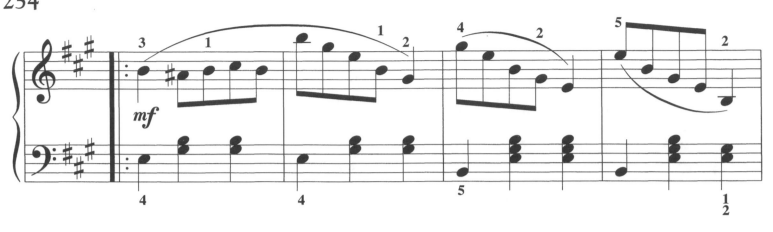

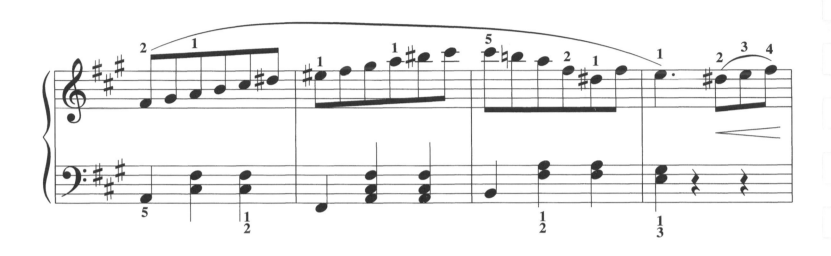

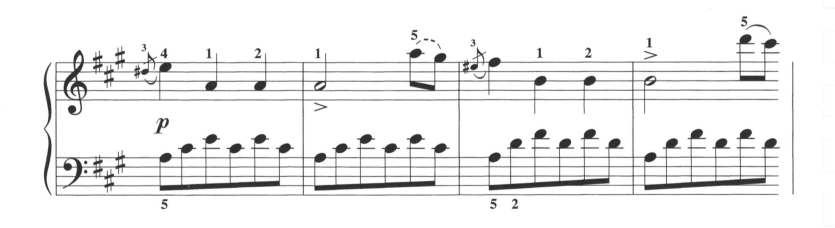

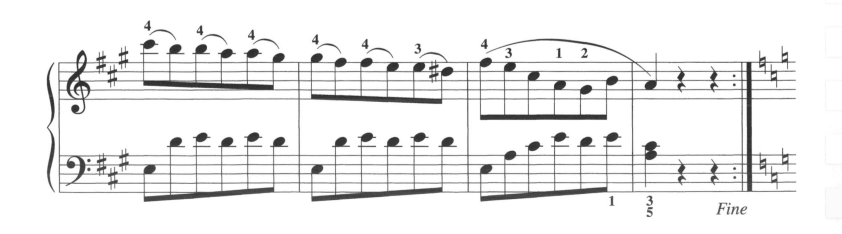

INDEX